The Peacocks of Baboquivari

ERMA J. FISK

The Peacocks of Baboquivari

Illustrations by Louise Russell

W · W · NORTON & COMPANY · NEW YORK · LONDON

Permission to reprint material used on the following pages is gratefully acknowledged:

Page 92: From *Prayers from the Ark* by Carmen Bernos de Gasztold. First published under the title *Le Mieux Aime* and *Prieres dans l'Arche*. Copyright 1947, 1955 by Editions du Cloitre. English text copyright © 1962 by Rumer Godden. Reprinted by permission of Viking Penguin Inc.

Page 184: From *The Creatures' Choir* by Carmen Bernos de Gasztold. First published under the title *Choral de Betes*. Copyright 1960, 1965 by Editions du Cloitre. English text copyright © 1965 by Rumer Godden. Reprinted by permission of Viking Penguin Inc.

Page 198: From *Our Natural World* by Hal Borland. Reprinted by permission of Barbara Dodge Borland. Copyright © 1965 by Hal Borland.

Pages 228–29: From *Woman in Levi's* by Eulalia Bourne. Copyright 1967 by the University of Arizona Press, Tucson. Reprinted by permission.

Page 273: From *Countryman: A Summary of Belief* by Hal Borland. Reprinted by permission of Barbara Dodge Borland. Copyright © 1965 by Hal Borland.

Published simultaneously in Canada by George J. McLeod Limited, Toronto
Printed in the United States of America

The text of this book is composed in V.I.P. Garamond, with
display type set in Cochin Italic. Composition and
manufacturing by The Maple-Vail Book Manufacturing Group.
Book design by Antonina Krass

First Edition

Library of Congress Cataloging in Publication Data
Fisk, Erma J.
The peacocks of Baboquivari.
Includes index.
1. Birds—Arizona—Thomas Canyon.   I. Title.
QL684.A6F57 1983   598.29791'77   83-2271

ISBN 0-393-01758-3

W. W. Norton & Company, Inc., 500 Fifth Avenue, New York, N.Y. 10110
W. W. Norton & Company Ltd., 37 Great Russell Street, London WC1B 3NU

1 2 3 4 5 6 7 8 9 0

Papago Myth of Baboquivari

Iitoi, known as Elder Brother, came down from Baboquivari and took the red clay from his mother the Earth, and formed man. He made the head first so that man might be wise. When he finished, he put the forms in the hot sun to bake. Then Iitoi went back up to Baboquivari to unleash the wind that lived in the cave on the sacred mountain

Above Baboquivari a large dark cloud formed, and moved down the mountain. A wind blew over the man and lifted the mold up. It looked as if it might blow away, but the wind stopped. The man sat up and looked around. Iitoi greeted him and told man that he was the child of earth, sun, and wind He cautioned the man not to harm the earth or she would cease to give him all the things he needed.

The land we save is a living legacy. It is held in trust forever, our gift to succeeding generations.

The Nature Conservancy

Introduction

Dear My Sponsors:

As you will see, I am neither The Perfect Observer nor the Meticulous Scribe. If it is any comfort I am as dissatisfied as you.

While these records were carefully compiled, it was by a propane lamp or candlelight. They had to be typed in scrips and scraps on fading ribbons, and as time allowed. They suffered in the process, and also were under the control of a headstrong typewriter (Any tendency to being headstrong in the typist would rapidly have been destroyed by the terrain and the weather.)

I will send a detailed Report of my data for your files. This condensed account, following, is my formal, final

REPORT TO THE NATURE CONSERVANCY

From December 21, 1978, to May 5, 1979, a study was made documenting the birds of the Conservancy property at the head of Thomas Canyon, Pima County, Arizona. This ranch comprises 640 acres. The buildings are at an elevation of 4,500

feet, approximately one and a half airmiles east of Baboquivari
Peak. Known as Riggs Ranch on the Coast and Geodetic Survey maps, it is bordered by lands under the jurisdiction of the
U.S. Bureau of Land Management and the State Land Department. It had been in private hands, its natural history had not
been studied.

Mist nets, increasing from three to eighteen, were used to
catch the birds. Three traps were baited daily. The need for
frequently checking the nets precluded their being set more
than a half-mile distant. However, observations by visitors
using the trails up the mountain and adjacent ridges added
few species to my personal list.

Activity was hampered for the first weeks by the presence of
ranch cats. Resident peacocks and ground squirrels proved a
disturbance to ground-feeding species. The dominant mesquite, leafless until April, provided no shade to camouflage
the nets. Those set under oaks were torn by cattle seeking
shade. In this remote area birds were unaccustomed to feeders
and not easily attracted to them.

Total net hours for the period number 7,555. Individuals
handled were 449, of 70 species. Another 25 species were
observed. One hundred seventy-four birds repeated more than
once from 318 recaptures. A *Selasphorus* female taken February
20th was a state record. U.S. Fish and Wildlife Service bands
were placed on all but hummingbirds under federal permit
#7081, Arizona permit #063. Birds were weighed, meas-
ured, examined for parasites, molt, and plumage. They were
aged and sexed as possible from information provided by the
Bird Banding Laboratory of the U.S. Fish and Wildlife Service. Some behavior was noted.

Acknowledgments

I wish to thank The Nature Conservancy for the opportunity they extended to me.

In Arizona I particularly thank Dr. Sally Hoyt Spofford, who encouraged and supported this manuscript from its beginning, and her husband, Dr. Walter R. Spofford. William G. Roe of the Arizona Conservancy, Dr. G. Scott Mills, Assistant Curator of Birds at the University of Arizona, and their wives, with their interest and care, made my winter possible. I also thank Douglas and Kendall and Peggy Cumming, whose visits to the Ranch and whose courtesy buoyed my sometimes flagging spirits; and Herman Mayer, who was a true friend. On the east coast Robert Finch and James L. Mairs for their editorial support and Louise Russell for her illustrations have my forever friendship.

ARIZONA

mist net
XXXXXX

trail
to
Baboquivari

MEXICO

1 Tucson
2 Three Points
3 Green Valley
4 Tumacacori
5 Sonoita
6 Nogales
7 Arivaca
8 Sasabe
9 Riggs Ranch ~ Thomas Canyon
10 Kitts Peak

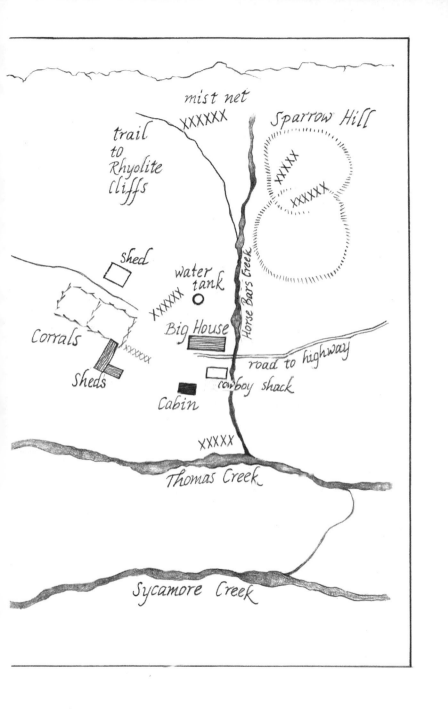

The Peacocks of Baboquivari

December 12th. Sky overcast to sunny. No wind.
Temperature 67 degrees at 1600 Navy time
(4:00 P.M. in my social life)

With final encouraging *abrazos*—

"What's an *abrazo?*" my Harvard granddaughter, Molly, asked me, reading this.

"A hug. Don't you know Mexican?" I slanted my eyes at her. She comes from California. She knows all about *abrazos*, too. Under another name.

All right, start again.

The two men who have transported me and my gear for five months embrace me, climb into their yellow Wagoneer, and head for the paved road ten miles distant. Cautiously they negotiate the first washout, lurch, then disappear around a jutting hill. I strain to hear their motor. I keep myself from running after them, around the bend to see them—just once more, even just their backs jouncing away. Out of sight, out of sound. There is only the wind lifting the hair on my neck, the blood singing in my ears. I am alone. Quite reasonably I panic.

All my sheltered life I have been fascinated by stories of

women who man fire towers, live on islands, in lighthouses on fogbound coasts, in wilderness cabins. Wondering what it would be like, wishing to do it. It occurs to me now, joltingly, that always they have had a sturdy man—a ranger, husband, supervisor, a friendly neighbor with strong arms and protective instincts, to support them. I have no one. Seventy-three years old, seventy-five miles from city, friends, stores. No communication. My car two miles down canyon. A city woman with an arthritic shoulder, a gimpy hip, no resourceful abilities. How crazy can I be? How did I get into this?

The facts are that it is December 12th. I stand at an altitude of 4,500 feet in the Upper Austral Life Zone in the Baboquivari foothills of Arizona, southwest of Tucson, thirty miles south of Kitts Peak observatory, fifteen miles north of Mexico. Biome Southern Desert Scrub, coordinates 314–1113. This ranch, Riggs Ranch on the Coast and Geodetic Survey maps, had been homesteaded in 1920 by a Texas cowboy. It was bought ten years ago by two brothers Cumming who used it only for running cattle, not for living. Last summer they sold it to The Nature Conservancy. I'll get into all this later, if anyone is interested. At the moment I am just looking at it. Nervously.

All about me, steep up, steep down, are mesquite and grassland foothills that rise on either side of Thomas Canyon. The Canyon and the hills mount to a forested saddleback. This in turn rises to the great rectangular slab of Baboquivari Peak, a mile and a half airmiles distant. Three thousand feet above me. The air is so clear I can almost touch it—well, the air is mighty clear. No belching smokestacks, no carbon monoxide, no truck-noisy highways.

The Peak itself is on the Papago Indian Reservation. Its granite face is a palette of colors shifting in the late afternoon

December sun. From the base of that thousand-foot slab down we own this side. (You see how quickly I have taken possession. We, indeed!) We and the Department of State Lands and the U. S. Bureau of Land Management, who plan to buy our 640 acres when they get the funds. The Indians I can't see—they live on the other side, around Ajo—believe that their gods reside in the remote and harsh beauty of this awesome rock. They guard it zealously, so that hikers and climbers and naturalists of all kinds use the Ranch for access—one reason The Conservancy bought it. I am hoping more every moment, as I become increasingly conscious of silence, that those high gods will watch over my paleface incompetence as I stumble about their terrain. I have already discovered that bifocals make the rocky footing precarious.

The hills (mountains to my eastern eyes) are sprinkled with Blue and Emory oaks, streaked with thin lines of arroyos and small canyons. These are delineated by hackberry, Arizona walnut, more oaks, and occasionally on the flats by a few sycamores. (I studied up on this botanical information while I was in Tucson, I wouldn't know a hackberry from an elm.) Oaks (I do know those) are everywhere dominant, but higher—I'll never make it there—are pines. More or less to the north looms a fissured wall of rhyolite. (I never did figure out the compass lines what with the seasonal tilting of our planet, and the slopes skewing my sun and moon out of line, the hills blocking their rise and fall. For twelve years I have been living on the wide flat of South Florida where you can *see* where you are.) This is pale now in the fading light, but golden in full sun, sharp and forbidding on gray days. Golden eagles (which are dark brown) fly along its face sometimes.

Below me the ground drops sharply to Thomas Creek, brawling from unseasonal rains, then rises as sharply to ridges that block my view of Mexico. My lifeline is to the east, down where that yellow four-wheel drive has gone, along the Creek. It is a winding mile to the first ford and its windmill, another rockier mile to the second ford, on the far side of which my VW—I hope—sits under a thorn tree. Beyond this the Creek canyon opens to a valley, the valley hills slope to the flat Altar Desert, and my lifeline finally reaches the highway. Ten miles, a small voice inside me whispers. I'm told there is a ranch seven miles south of this, if I get in trouble. A long walk. . . . From our entrance the highway runs south to Sasabe on the Mexican border, north to Three Points where you turn east toward Tucson. Three Points because of three roads meeting. Robles Junction if you are a purist, or travel by map.

This is all so glorious to behold, so stimulating, that I forget my panic. I am standing in an open space where visitors can nose their cars between bushes, if there aren't more than three (cars). Downhill, between me and the Ranch buildings, water rushing and tumbling from the Rhyolite Cliffs has gouged a narrow gully. Vehicles can cross this if they don't mind damaging their tailpipes. Jumping from rock to rock I get wet crossing it. I climb through horse bars and walk up to the Big House in a cleared space that is the Ranch—yard I suppose you would call it, unless yard to you means an orderly open area with mowed grass and shrubs. There *are* shrubs—a great clump of Mexican bamboo, massive and sere, and a curving wall of gray-green agave, lethally tipped. An ancient yellow truck sags by an equally sagging outbuilding. There is an antique metal swing, a long rusty barbecue, a corral, piles of rotting lumber. On either side of the Big House with its narrow pillared porch and woodpile are neglected, fenced gardens.

I explore. In a bunkhouse where cowboys coming up to ride fence presumably stay I find tack and decrepit sofas and furniture and a stove and paint. Then the clearing slants (nothing here is level) down to the original homestead, which is my winter home—a small rock cabin with a woodshed at one end of a small porch, dry vines rustling on its walls. Water pipes and rocks emerge from the hardpacked soil so the footing is uneven (to be polite). Doghouses with stakes and chains, trash barrels, decrepit animal and chicken pens ornament my personal yard. Out back Bill Roe, my Conservancy sponsor, my host for these last ten cold and rainy days we have spent in Tucson waiting for the weather to clear, had proudly shown me a hot-water heater. Hurrah! By now those two men in their yellow Wagoneer must have reached the highway and be barreling north. They were reluctant to leave me. Why? I am having a fine time.

Bill couldn't turn the heater on, his wife Alice is the family mechanic, and she didn't come. Beside it, onto a square of cement, leaks a shower. Beside that an ancient refrigerator holds soap and shaving materials. This yard ends at what was once a vegetable garden. Long ago. Chives still survive in it, I am pleased to see. Thomas Creek brawls beyond an outhouse. My grandmother had a three-holer out back when I was little. It grew the most luxuriant thicket of fragrant privet and huge sunflowers a small child could imagine. I'll bet that privet was full of catbirds, but it was forty years before I learned what was a catbird. My grandmother also had an iron pump by her well, with Dorothy Perkins roses climbing the lattice. It was my proud young job to pull on a wooden pump handle to fill the buckets for the kitchen. I loved that pump and its roses and wooden sluice. I had a happy childhood.

Back to your survey, Fisk. My new home sounds grubby? It isn't. If the human residue in view is deshabille it is not really disorderly, and its effect against the overpowering, many-hued splendor of "my" mountain is picayune. Whatever is this clutter of pots and pans scattered about? Tomorrow they go. My eyes slide over and discard them. Do YOU notice the power lines and road signs and billboards and gas stations that are YOUR daily fare as you drive into town? Any U.S. town? If the trees are December bare the Mexican jays calling in them are flashing blue. Wondering, no doubt, if I am good for a handout. On a pole that dangles old electric lines above the bamboo thicket a Say's phoebe perches, and then darts out after its supper. Those huge agave curving along the way to the Big House are a soft gray-green, like silk, almost a sea color. Everywhere is a magnificence that will take me weeks to absorb. The grinding roar of the Creek is exciting. I can see where last spring's flash flood, the one that washed out the just-repaired road, left debris thirteen feet up in the trees along its banks, and undercut the hill by the old barn.

As I say, I can ignore any clutter, or clear some of it up. Then I burst into laughter and forget it. I am not alone after all in this quiet mountain fastness. Stepping irregularly out from bamboo and agave, from under Rancher's Wife's over-grown Talisman rosebush, coming to inspect *me* is a flock of peacocks! Five thousand feet up on an arid desert mountain-side, in the realm of the Papago Indian gods—PEACOCKS! Ignoring me, the two cocks posture and rattle their quills. Ignoring them, the hens peck placidly at the dirt. A white, half-grown hybrid skulks to one side. Plummeting from a tree arrives a Bantam rooster in flaming red and orange plumage, to strut before me. I have my personal, resident barnyard animals! Varmints must get eggs and chicks each spring, but nine of these incongruous birds have survived over the years and with a great show of indifference THEY are assessing ME.

What was it Rancher Brother had said when I had commented uncertainly that perhaps I am too old to handle living in this isolation? That a woman even older had been here for years, ranch-sitting for them, without even a car to get to town for groceries? Obviously she had kept hens—I now see, under vines, that coops and a henyard have been wired against skunks and owls. Somewhere in the valley I should be able to restock them (hens; skunks will come by themselves). Hens are comfortable company, undemanding. And they lay eggs. I am going to weary of canned food. In my mind's eye, along with hens I see herbs and lettuce and tomatoes growing among the iris and hollyhock shoots of the old gardens. Watching the peacocks preen and feed, I compare the ludicrousness of this new habitat to our comfortable home full of children in Buffalo; to our Georgetown row house in Washington; to the small cottage that has housed my last thirteen widowed years in Florida, with its citrus trees, flowers, heron stalking in the pond I had made for my bird studies. This wipes out any tinge of depression, of a fright that has begun as the sun disappears so early over the empty ridges.

The small porch of the cabin I must cram myself into is strewn with the cartons and suitcases and water jugs and books the men so cheerfully unloaded a few hours ago, pushing them

23

aside for room to enjoy our sandwiches and beer in the sun. I enter the cabin and find a broom. At heart I am a nester, a housewife. My ornithological career budded only after my man's death, when the world of people had been too close, too abrasive for me to reenter.

What am I doing up here, isolated on this mountain with no neighbors, no telephone or CB, not even electricity? No one dropping in for coffee or beer and a chat? Mail not arriving sometimes for two weeks? My larder stocked with dried beans, dried milk, rice, raisins, prunes, canned applesauce, tomatoes, hash? It's what everyone asks, so maybe I should explain.

I am here to document for The Nature Conservancy the bird life of this remote property. I will do this for them by field observation, and by banding, photographing, and then releasing birds I hope to trap, or to capture in mist nets.

A mist net is about the length of a tennis net, but is five tiers high, stretched as far as I can reach up to extricate a bird. It is made of fine nylon mesh, and comes in different sizes depending upon whether you wish to catch hawks or hummingbirds. I use the all-purpose size and have caught *everything*, from hummingbirds to Red-shouldered hawks; as well as snakes, insects, large butterflies and moths (which with enormous patience I can extract), dragonflies (nearly impossible; the fine net strands catch under the plates of their heads, or they bite on them and won't let go. Dragonflies bite people too; it hurts as well as surprises). To my dismay I have had chipmunks in my nets, though rarely a gray squirrel; a box turtle and the sign of raccoons, fox, possum, cats, dogs, and people.

A bander must have a special license and training to use nets. Birds that get in can be taken out, but if you leave them for any length of time they can get tangled, so I don't. Legs might be hurt, wings sprained. It makes me nervous to see a beginner handling them. But then, 40,000 birds ago I was a beginner, and clumsy also.

Preferably nets are placed in shade, between shrubs or low trees that will obscure them. You must clear lanes for this with clippers, machete, sweat, often an axe, wide enough so that wind will not catch or tear the net on thorns or branches. (Nets are expensive.) You are careful not to wear clothes with buttons or zippers that will snag in them. You close nets in rain, or at night to avoid predation by the above creatures, and you don't leave them unattended for any length of time. When not in use they are rolled up tightly, furled as you would furl a sail, then fastened—by me at any rate—with a few clothespins.

They were invented by the Japanese, I have been told, at first woven from their women's long black hair. They were brought to this country in the 1950s by Dr. Oliver L. Austin, Jr., who was raised on the Cape Cod property where recent summers I have given banding demonstrations (plus all the conservation message I can work in) for the Massachusetts Audubon Society. The world is small. I banded Sooty terns with Oliver on the Dry Tortugas, catching them on their nests with a big butterfly net. He was far less frightening than his reputation, all those letters and honors after his name. I tell you, banding gets you to wonderful places, with wonderful people.

Birds have extraordinarily sharp vision and reflexes. Again and again I have watched them swoop up over a net at the very last moment—or down under, or around, or through a hole. A proportion of birds in an area, and over a period of time probably all of the residents, are caught. When a bird does fly into the net its weight sags the mesh, making a pocket, and your victim—usually—is held by wing or head or clutching feet—the latter making its removal slow, as you loosen them talon by talon. Most lie quietly until the bander approaches. Heavy-bodied ones like doves, jays, and small hawks may bounce along the length of the net and out the end—often just as I am reaching for them. Small species like wrens, hummers, some warblers may wiggle through, but most remain to regard me with a wary eye, hammer on my fingers with sharp bills, peck my hands.

If it is windy you do not—should not—net, as wind can strangle a fine strand around a throat. If it is cold a bird becomes too chilled. If it is too hot, birds may not survive exposure to the midday sun, or heat reflected from rocky soil. If it is rainy feathers stick to your fingers and are detached. Birds need their feathers. So you use care, I have had some accidents. But no more—not as many—as the window kills at suburban homes. How many birds do you pass dead along roadsides? Particularly in the north, where salt is lavished on icy highways and species like the spectacular grosbeaks come down for it? How many birds does a feral cat kill? (A feral cat, usually, is a once charming kitten turned loose at the end of summer. Those that survive become very, very smart, and of course are always hungry. They are not taken in by traps.)

I get upset when I talk about dead birds. We don't have that many live ones any more. How many birds (wild ones, not sparrows and starlings) at a suburban shopping plaza that used to be woods or pasture or marsh? How many young emerge from highway borders and utility rights-of-way sprayed—always in breeding season—to keep down vegetation? There are other ways to handle vegetation than spraying—ask the state of Connecticut. What happens to birds you have trained to come to your window feeders when you go away, even if only for a few days, in midwinter? What is the effect of the forest destruction in Central and South America, so rapidly depleting the wintering grounds of many of our migrants?

I can go on for hours about this. I often do, holding a bird in my hand for my audience to study. When released it leaves with a few equally well-chosen words of its own, flies over our heads, perches on a branch, realigns its feathers, investigates that shiny new bracelet.

I have left The Conservancy hanging. I was explaining why I am here.

"The Nature Conservancy is a national conservation organization committed to preserving natural diversity by finding and protecting areas that contain the best samples of all components of the natural world. . . . Forests, wetlands, prairies, mountains and islands—refuges for threatened wildlife and rare plants, places of special beauty remain untouched and protected because The Conservancy and its members cared and acted quickly." I am quoting from their brochure.

A branch of The Conservancy is centered in Tucson. Its Arizona Heritage program, sparked by my new friend and sponsor, Bill Roe, is a cooperative effort with the state government "to identify imperiled habitat and natural systems before these resources are lost."

"Woe to those who join house to house, who add field to field until there is not a place where they may be alone." Isaiah wrote that long ago, aware even in those less populated days of man's spiritual need for space left natural, green, empty.

I have volunteered to live on this Ranch, protecting it, finding out what birds are resident in winter, what birds come through and when, in spring migration. I was looking at a handful of *Arizona Highways* and travel folders when I involved myself in this.

Somewhere is a carbon I sent Sally Spofford of my original letter to Bill Roe. It was written on an idle summer day when I was wondering if there mightn't be somewhere more useful for me to work during the winter than Florida. I don't keep letters, but Sally does. She has filled cabinets with them over the years, God knows why (or how she has the time). She and Spoff are old friends from my Cornell Laboratory of Ornithology days. They retired to the Chiricahuas in Arizona. Literally hundreds of people a year beat a path to their kitchen to see the extraordinary birds and extraordinary numbers of hummingbirds they have attracted to their yard at Cave Creek Canyon, along with panhandling bob- and ring-tailed cats and peccary (called in Arizona by their Mexican name of javelina). They admit all these people, friends or strangers, give them coffee, Kleenex, directions, and cheer. They have been trying to lure me to Arizona for years. I don't want busloads of eager bird listers hammering at my door; I am the solitary type. Here, I found it, the letter. Undated, probably September:

"If you know of a cabin in a canyon where an old crone is needed to count hummingbirds and tanagers outside the window I might easily be tempted. I can think of a dozen reasons why not, but then I have never been a reasonable woman. I'm not as young as in 1945 when I first visited Arizona, and I am not a real ornithologist, just a pseudo, with probably only two or three more years to dig out useful data. So this is only a dream, but thank you for suggesting it. I've always lived by water, so the first thing I would do would be to dig a pool, even if it had to be filled with gingerale, and wait for a pelican. A White one, it would be, in Arizona."

Letter to Bill Roe, September 14th

"I definitely heard you gulp over the telephone. Never mind, I was gulping too.

"My father taught me that men always know best, so I will travel as you advised, from D. C. via Phoenix, American Airlines Flight 115, Friday, arriving at 7:34 P.M. Unless the airlines change schedules first and screw everything up. I will depart Sunday at 7:55 A.M. This fixes it so, I hope, I don't interfere with your gainful occupations, and so your spouse won't have to feed me dinner or breakfast. And so you will have the whole day Sunday to spend with your family. And so I return to D.C. in time to see my grandchildren there, who seem only to be home on Sunday afternoons, and at supper time, if then. Wait till you have teen-agers. . . . This also gives me excursion rates.

"Actually I don't need to come at all. A pig in a poke would be more exciting, but I judge you are a conservative lawyer and would be happier if I looked the situation over first. I am sure I should, although I am a great leaper before looking. I'll study up on flycatchers. I sent my good binoculars to Germany last month for repair. Because I wouldn't be needing them. Oho. Does all this scare you? It does me."

Perhaps, dear Reader, this explains why I am sitting by candlelight at a dark window; how I ever got myself into this venture. It seems normal to me. If a door opens you go through it. Then there is another door. Sometimes it needs a brisk kick if you are to get through, but not too often. Life is like a Christmas stocking. You will find soap and toothpaste and apples (in my family we did), but usually there is a shiny coin, perfume, a small mysterious box also. Once as a small girl I found lumps of coal and ran crying, to hide in a cupboard. Life can do this to you, too. You take it as it comes.

Letter to the Spoffords, September 19th

"I have had rats and bats and bees and scorpions and spiders and termites in my walls in one home or another, and our California son has two pairs of raccoons breeding in his, so I suppose I can adjust to the *metades* that you refer to you in your recent zany epistle, but what are they? I don't mind having no telephone, I don't mind being isolated. I can live on tortillas and tuna fish, and I have *lots* of scruffy clothes. What else do you know about my future home?

"Another day, like Thursday.
"Oho, you non-bilingual woman—*metates!* I *do* know what they are. I asked Bill what was running around in the Ranch house walls. I may say he sounded flummoxed when I phoned, but he rallied. I am seriously considering coming out. My electric typewriter doesn't run on propane so I wouldn't have to write letters all winter. Whoops! Judging from your life at Cave Creek Canyon, as soon as word gets around that a Lady Bander is in residence in Thomas Canyon, just as soon as I catch one Mexican bird, I will have visitors like bees. Bill warns I must bring my supplies all the way from Tucson so I will hang a sign on the gate reading *No Admittance Without Coffee, Food, and Paper Goods.* My sister does beautiful script, I can set her to work on this.

"Bill insists I fly out to see what I am getting into. Of

course I may not like it (I'm already half packed). If I had seen Homestead before I moved to Florida I would never have gone there. What worries me more than the distance of the Ranch from Tucson is that I may not live up to William's expectations. I am willing to WORK, but you know I am not all that good. Will you explain this to him? On the other hand I am overjoyed at the prospect of being somewhere I *can* work, instead of just picking oranges and running around with an axe trying to keep that terrible Florida holly the birds love cut back enough so I can drive up my rutted lane.

"I leave for Maine in the morning. I had better wash my hair and get ready. Did you find a busload of birdwatchers at your gate on arrival? How do you put up with all those chattering people in your kitchen? If Bill sets me up near you, I can take some of the heat off you. Maybe. Of course this is why I am coming to Arizona . . ."

December 13th

The peacocks woke me at first light (7:15), stamping on my roof. At noon the Cummings arrived, bringing up cattle for winter grazing—Rancher Doug, Wife Peggy, Rancher Brother Kendall, a son, and Herman the Cowboy, a retiree from Kodak. They fed me pumpkin pie—yum; turned on my hot-water heater and fridge; and bandaged broken water lines with rubber tubing. They had had trouble at a washout, and had passed hikers hung up on a boulder (not the hikers, their truck). They promised me the Road Repair Man would soon appear, although not this week. After the hunting season. After Christmas. January. I have lots of canned goods, and work to do; I can last. They left, Herman stayed. I hiked up the Canyon at dusk and saw my first deer, silhouetted against the sky. They seemed as curious about me, bundled in my red jacket and beret, as I about them. A soft gray sky stretched into infinity between the V of the valley hills, like my Atlantic Ocean in a mist. No, I am not homesick. Yet. This is only my first day.

December 13th. Round-robin letter to my children

Riggs Ranch, Thomas Canyon
Pima County, Arizona
Not an address

"Hi, Everyone, I have arrived! I had a neat Thanksgiving week in California with all your relatives, eating myself out of shape up and down the Peninsula. Back in Tucson it kept raining and was damned cold, so Bill wouldn't bring me up. Yesterday I told him if he didn't, I was going back to your Aunt Win's. He has eighteen irons in the fire and some place he must be every day from now to New Year's; I could see myself parked on a strange family forever, however hospitable and cheerful, however many midnights I was licking envelopes for them, trying to earn my keep. I was restive to get to *my* work. They were mailing out an appeal for the Arizona Nature Conservancy—four thousand letters! I helped address and sort them. At midnight, teetering on ladders and walls, we harvested their tangerine tree when the Sun Belt temperature dropped below freezing for the third night in a row. I squeezed bushels of the fruit for Alice. She was crawling around on the floor, bundling envelopes into zip codes and shoe boxes. At least I could work standing up.

"So we came. My VW Wagon could get only partway up to the Ranch. I was terrified by the cattle track Arizonans consider a road, once you leave the highway. I drove gingerly in Bill's every tire mark, praying. Two miles down Canyon the men had to trans-ship me and my baggage. We had lunch in the sun, they hugged me and left. Water pipes broken. Fridge not turned on (Bill is not mechanical and Scott is a biologist.) But there is an outhouse, and a water pipe beside my small cabin spurted a fountain fine for washing in, and for catching water for cooking. Scenery stupendous! I can live on that for a while.

"The cabin was tidy, with a lamp, matches, two tin plates, a mug, a skillet, mouse tracks wiped off all the surfaces. I tried operating by candlelight but found it onerous. Was too tired to experiment with my new propane lantern, or to search for the batteries for another I had bought, because if one light gives out, seventy-five miles from town you need another, right? It was dark by 5:30. There are two lonely cats that try to come in the door every time I open it. And a flock of PEA-COCKS, for Pete's sake!

"I am not alone. Rancher and Wife appeared briefly at noon today. They tried to give me a hound dog with topaz eyes and liver spots, but I refused him. Said they would remove the two wild Ranch cats the next time they come up. Two weeks! Oh dear! How can I trap birds with cats around? Herman the Cowboy went away with them but later reappeared in a German-tidy blue jeep. He is said to be very good at fixing things. Wonder if he can squeeze the heap of unpacked goods and chattels still in the middle of my floor into some order?

"The weather has been the coldest on record. Below zero in Nogales—Nogales!—In Portal, where I almost had gone back to stay with the Spoffords again it was 7 degrees, with seven inches of snow. Power out, pipes frozen. Various friends in Tucson came by before I left with down quilts for me, and jackets and lined gloves and worried looks. I just hope I won't need these! A tiny iron stove that burns mesquite does an excellent job of heating my one room. If I calculate carefully I can cook on it too—two small pans for soup, and beans or coffee. There is also a normal stove (well, it looks normal; it has a mouse nest in it) that takes up a lot of room. Propane. And a big propane fridge that Rancher lit for me.

"Few birds. Wandering cattle, horses, and those darn peacocks may be a problem with my netting. Every view is gorgeous. No sound except cats meowing at my door, the Creek rolling boulders downstream, and wind rushing through the Canyon. No telephone. It's marvelous! Love to all."

December 14th

At 6:30 A.M. in this canyon pocket the sky is gray. A gibbous moon drops slowly through mesquite branches. Somewhere the Bantam rooster crows. At 7:12 the last yellow glimmer of moon blinks and is gone behind the slope of a steep hill across the Creek. Trying to scramble up that hill to photograph yesterday I found it no "hill" to eastern legs. It will be another hour before the sun shows over the steep slopes to the east. I lie in bed a little longer with the excuse that I must hoard my lamp. Until the road is repaired I must pack in my supplies from the further side of two fords. Two miles. A long, uphill haul. The fords are a jumble of rocks and gullies.

The cats run on the roof overhead. They are large, affectionate animals, left with a supply of food when Rancher and Wife come up, to run wild. They are sitting at the door when I go out in my nightgown to read the thermometer, to know how to dress. They follow me all day, like dogs, to certain cat-determined distances. Until they are removed I cannot set out my nets or operate traps.

One had to find out what things were not necessary, what things one really needed. A little music and liquor, still less food, a warm and beautiful but not too big roof of one's own, a channel for one's creative energies and love, the sun and the moon.

—T. H. White, *The Goshawk*

My cabin is in order. It has to be. Twenty by sixteen feet (my feet). A huge bed won't budge out from the rough rock wall, so it is hell to make. Comfortable, though. Through the windows at its head wind slips readily. A dinette table will serve for desk and eating. A glass-fronted city bookcase tidily houses papers, desk supplies, camera, recorder, candles, and other needs. Its wide top is useful (for books). An ancient overstuffed chair is good for dumping things on, piled high at the moment; not for reading—there is no light near it, nor place for a lamp. Windowsills are handy for tools, apples, mousetraps, carrots, more books, general spillover. Someone—Herman?—cobbled a narrow table for pots and pans, flour and sugar bins, the big breadbox I bought to store mouse-attractants in—perhaps even space to slice bread and set the lamp so I can see to cook at night? The sink is too small to hold a skillet, much less a dishpan. There is a dishpan, though; I found it wedged under the sink trap. For a reason. Until Herman came running to my anguished call the faucet poured water through the drain and overflowed it onto all my carefully arranged groceries in the cupboard below.

I expect the floor needed washing anyway.

Over the sink is the cabin's only shelf, ingeniously hung from the ceiling by ropes. At one end I have decoratively stood, anchored with thumbtacks, three plates, and set three pretty cocktail glasses—*lares penates* I carry about with me for a Touch of Home. At the other end are lined up cereals and dry goods in which mice rustled happily last night. The mugs and cups I bought, with great good luck they harmonize with the orange in the rocks of my wall, can be hung under this when I get to town for hooks. All very tidy. There is no way of getting light at the sink evenings, or even much in the daytime, I will have to clean my dishes by feel. No matter. No one but me will be eating from them.

"A place for everything, and everything in its place," as Gene Knoder is always admonishing his wife Grace, infuriating her. If ever I expect to find it again. There is little room for walking between the file boxes I haven't yet dealt with, but these can wait for a rainy day. I shove and pile them under the table to clear room for the Mexican rug Gene once gave me, with birds on it. Of course I brought a rug! This is my HOME, I am not camping. For five months? Gene and Sandy Sprunt and I once flew in a small plane around the Gulf of Mexico, from Key West to Belize City, censusing waterbird colonies for National Audubon. Low over the then wild marshes of the Mexican coast (now tamed and black with oil) we saw jabirus, and a solid mile of Wood storks nesting. A mile of solid Wood storks? How do you say that? A breathtaking sight, however the grammar. As were the jabirus.

Getting a nail in a rock wall is not easy, but I have managed to hang a painting of sunrise on the Atlantic to remind me of where I come from, and an enormous photograph of Least terns brooding young. I have worked many years to get protection for these small, sand-nesting birds, threatened in coastal states by human pressures on their beaches, in desperation now breeding on supermarket and department store roofs, so this is suitable, if somewhat surprising in its desert setting. It rode up from Tucson wrapped against the jolts and swerves in a big quilt. Bought as a decorative bed cover, glowing burnt orange in the dark cabin, this quilt proved a godsend. Spread over my Hudson's Bay blanket it kept me snug all winter.

The story—or legend—of my cabin is that Riggs, the original homesteader, was a Texas cowboy on the lam. He rode into this high Canyon, fell in love with it (or found safety in its remoteness), worked on the new road reaching down to Sasabe to afford building materials, trekked them up by mule-cart. He prospered, built the Big House and its outbuildings and water tanks, corrals and gardens, equipped them with electricity and a good road to service the many friends he entertained. He collected, as well as friends, a vast store of *metates*—Indian grinding stones—and incorporated many into his walls, both outside and in. The legend says that eventually when he retired to Tucson he took two—or three—truckloads of them with him. He also, legend again, gave a Farewell Party for two hundred, says one Cumming brother; three hundred, says the other (two or three seem to be the numbers associated with him). The long barbeque rusting in the yard would handle either. It is said he served roast peacock. Hmmmmm. At any rate, he was the one who brought in those damned birds whose droppings I walk in all day. His buildings and gates and grounds and definitely his road have fallen into disrepair, although with a liberal use of baling wire and rubber strips all but the last are still serviceable.

The Rancher Brothers, Doug and Kendall Cumming, alternate coming up occasional weekends. Doug, who works a ranch near Nogales, calls one of the two horses running free on the hills, and checks cattle, fences, and for sign of mountain lion. Kendall, head of the State Bureau of Indian Affairs, drives the long way from Phoenix and also rides, I expect doing the same more casually; then sits, enjoying the sun and the peace. Both of them are solicitous for my comfort. Rancher's wife, Peggy, works like a demon in her few hours here, hosing down the porch, pruning and watering what garden has survived. She feeds her men, offers to feed me, fusses about peacock predation on tender flower buds. I am to prevent this. How? Have you ever argued with a peacock?

Much of the above, naturally, is not apparent or known to me that first evening, as I stumble around cartons in the shadows of my flashlight lantern. The men had put my propane lamp together for me—a good thing, the instructions were wholly inadequate—but I am scared to use it. They had also laid a fire in the tiny iron stove, but thought it best, I surmise, not to mention how cold the Canyon would be after sundown. The size of my woodpile should have warned me.

December 15th

I am living in clover. Herman is still here. He knows where there is a hawk's nest. He enjoys the Bewick's wren that slips in and out of the Big House through some crevice, its "mess" annoying Peggy. He repairs, tidies up, chops kindling, works on the hoses that run from the big water tank behind the corral.

"No need to worry about water," Rancher told me cheerfully. "Not until May. It has rained and rained."

My project for today is to pick up and scour or throw away all those kitchen pots, pans, and plastic dishes scattered about the yard.

"NO!" Herman says, finding me at this. "Those are for watering the peacocks."

I salvage a couple for my cooking, clean all of them and place them strategically, stepping everywhere in peacock —––— as I do so. I scrub the scum from a chicken trough green with algae and begin to understand the lack of small ground-feeding birds, the peacocks run them off. I discard the bottles of beauty aids and household helpers (furniture polish in a rock cabin?) left by my immediate predecessor. She was a short-lived resident, Herman tells me, young, appalled by the isolation. Lots of stove cleaner and obviously she never used it. I prowl through the Big House, and scrounge a low table and a better skillet—one whose handle doesn't twist in my hand. It is a pleasant 50 degrees, with a clear sky. No need for a fire in my stove, just a second sweater.

In the afternoon Bill appears briefly with Scott Mills, Assistant Curator of Birds at the University of Arizona, and my mail. A seventy-mile drive to make sure that I am surviving, that I really plan to stay. Bill insists on leaving me his new yellow Wagoneer in case I panic. He has me run it up and down through the gully of Horse Bars Creek until he is assured I can start and stop it and not tear off the tailpipe. He says if he shouldn't return I am expected in town for a dinner meeting December 21st, and they go swinging down the Canyon to take my VW in exchange.

Undated. Herman

Herman is more common around my dooryard than the jays. He has stayed on to check—on me also, I suspect—on the ards and yards of water lines that crisscross the ground, on the bandages of rubber that slow old leaks; to bring peacock grain and firewood, to repair, and to sit in the sun on his Big House porch, enjoying. He spends a lot of time sweeping that porch of peacock shit (all right, dung—but *you* don't step in it every other minute). A small, wiry man, he is in constant pain from a surgeon's blundering knife, but can outwalk me anytime. Being German, when he repairs something it is done right, and a background as pilot, police officer, and farmer and twenty-five years with Kodak enables him to fix almost anything. He has a wife down in the posh suburb of Green Valley, but he likes it better up here. When he mounts his ladder to his or my roof with tar bucket and broom the peacocks fly up with a rush of wings to sidewalk superintend. They LOVE to have Herman up on those roofs, high in the air like themselves. I LOVE to have Herman on my roof—with his every trip the cabin becomes more airtight and safe.

I sense his approval when he sees me sweeping my small porch and shaking out Gene's rug. My predecessor did not have this approval. Herman is my source of Ranch history. He likes his privacy, and respects mine, but does not object when I take him soup or gingerbread. Sometimes we sit over his coffee and listen to the weather on his radio; sometimes enjoy the afternoon sun on his porch while he deals with some balky equipment that I bring as an excuse to hear more stories. He has been telling me about Frances, who lived many years in my cabin. She was the one who kept chickens. He shot skunk

and other marauders for her. She was beloved by hikers and
ranchers, always having cookies and affection for them. Already
I have been asked about her. I don't have cookies—I am trying
to reduce my girth and am wary of that mousy stove—but I
hastily make coffee. Hikers have had enough of cheese and
apples, which are my staples also.

I am not sure Herman understands why I am here, but he
notices my general housewifely neatening up and drops unob-
trusive hints on how to manage in this new world. I am gen-
uinely grateful for his company, and surely couldn't get along
without his help. I haven't dated this entry, because he comes
and goes in his blue jeep, our friendship and his various tasks
have developed over the weeks.

I was not a birder until midlife. After our children were grown enough to be off all day at school or college we built a summer cottage on the Canadian shore of Lake Erie. Looking out the window one morning as I pulled on jeans, I jumped and cried out, "What's *that?*"

My husband was amused. "Don't you know a Great Blue Heron?"

And so with this ungainly tall creature began my introduction to the feathered denizens of our woods and beach. A neighbor put names on them for me, then conned me into becoming a bird bander for the U.S. Fish & Wildlife Service, wanting to learn if the chickadees he trapped at his cottage would fly in winter the third of a mile to my feeders. (The answere was NO.) Harold Mitchell, a blessed man who pushed raptor protection through the New York legislature, was writing a book on the birds of the Niagara Frontier and wanted documented records from my area. Both of these men recognized a patsy when they found one, which is how I came to be sitting at this window, writing as I watch Brown towhees venture in to feed among the peacocks. But if you think I am going to stop here you are wrong.

A government license to handle wild birds was easier to

come by in 1950 than it is now. Today you must have more
than time and enthusiasm, must serve an apprenticeship, be
making some special study. Of the some two thousand banders
the majority are government biologists working with game
birds and waterfowl; although now that birds are recognized
as environmental indicators, refuge men are showing more
interest and even obtaining funds to study and work with
dickey birds, which is how most game men loftily refer to
songbirds. Remember your childhood story of the canary that
let miners know their air was poisoned long before human
noses could detect the danger? Birds, with short lives, are
teaching us what pesticides, herbicides, oil in the ocean, pollutants of many sorts may also be doing to long-lived human
bodies. Birds and fish kills wave red flags at us, although we
don't often heed them. Birds are sensitive to many of the
chemicals we use so lavishly, spewing them from smokestacks
and tractors and airplanes and watering cans. The day I gath-
ered one hundred and twenty five killdeer from a tomato field
in south Florida, fresh dead from organophosphate spraying, I
had to wonder about the health of the inhabitants of an adjacent trailer park, about the small children who took still flapping birds home to try to help them. And about winter tourists
picking beans in the UPICK field a hundred yards away. Both
beans and human skins are porous, absorbing poison. DDT,
which we still export, proved to be the cause of the population
crash in osprey and eagle and peregrine falcons, at the head of
the avian food chain. Robins gave the first fatal signal on this,
researched, proved, by Joe Hickey (eminent ornithologist,
Professor of Ecology at the University of Wisconsin, a great
believer in Woman Power and a merry dinner companion).
Dickey birds are not as obvious as big raptors. Their small
dead or paralyzed bodies go unobserved in the woods, but they

are equally, or more, sensitive and are now used to monitor radiation and pollutants in research centers.

Birdwatchers, students, and nature photographers now outnumber duck hunters by far, and so have increasing economic and political clout. In 1975—and that was some years ago, before birdwatching became as fashionable and consuming an activity as it is now—government statistics on recreation figured that 49 million people spent 5 billion user-days observing wildlife. The word to note is *observing*—not shooting, or putting into creels and freezers. And 15 million photographers enjoyed 150 million user-days trying to take wildlife home to their living rooms on film. Add to this the economic benefit of bird books sold, binoculars, telescopes, backpacks, jackets, birdseed, bird carvings and prints and exhibitions, gasoline, motel rooms, airfare, and you see why both state and federal Game Commissions are changing their stance. However slowly.

Turning out by the hundred thousand for Christmas and May and Breeding Bird Censuses, birders report our songbirds diminishing, in some cases catastrophically. With small regard for our planet's future we cover over fields and woods and farms and streams with shopping malls, reservoirs, condominiums, thousands of miles annually of highways. We cut our forests for wood to send abroad, drench agricultural square miles with pesticides and acid rain that promptly move into our food chains. I wish I had a nickel for every paralyzed kestrel (that's the Sparrow hawk's most recent name) that was brought to me for care in Florida. If they survived I released them to feed again in the same fields or fruit groves on poison-sprayed insects. If you shoot geese or dove and serve them to guests at dinner, you might pause to think what may have coated the seeds they were feeding on. When you eat shellfish you might think about the loons and scoters, murres, dovekies, gulls, and other species found dying on our beaches from oil, or oiled vegetation or poisoned offal they have ingested, and wonder what shellfish and YOU ingest these days.

With the surge of interest in our planet since Carson's *Silent Spring* in 1962 and Earth Day in 1970, an increasing number of young people are making specialized studies in various aspects of ecology. Universities are turning out countless eager, bright students who write scientific papers, publish articles and photographs, work in refuges and parks and sanctuaries summers, in nature and research centers; who volunteer their spare time to Audubon, the Sierra Club, World Wildlife, Defenders of Wildlife, The Nature Conservancy, RARE— scores of similar conservation organizations that have sprung up all around the country. They are highly alert to environmental dangers and indicators.

Many of these researchers band birds. They may use streamers, wing markers, collars, tiny radios, dyes, and assortments of colored bands as well as the numbered ones issued by Fish & Wildlife. A proportion of amateurs like myself are backyard or weekend banders, over the years becoming semiprofessional. We all contribute to avian knowledge, if only in details of migration routes or longevity, speed of flight, notes on plumage or molt or behavior. You'd be surprised how little is known, how out of date textbooks are, how many questions I am asked we don't yet have answers for. *National Geographic* (to its astonishment, I was told) spent two years instead of two months researching the excellent article on bird migration they published in August 1979. (That's my Indigo Bunting on page 161, but I'll skip the story of how it got there. Just boast.) Since many of you may not read scientific journals I can tell you that birds are increasingly used to study the effects of our industrial technology, radiation, oil spills, red tides, and bird control at airports and garbage dumps, in the effort to preserve both their numbers and ours.

Anything an amateur can add to this information is useful. Each year Audubon publishes, in *American Birds,* a Blue List of threatened species. Pick your own kind—the list grows longer annually. The imported house finches, which now outnumber the imported house sparrows in some areas, have pushed out our native purple martins. The imported starling, an economic pest roosting by the hundred thousands on the buildings in our Nation's Capitol and elsewhere, drives out our native hole-nesters—woodpeckers, nuthatches, bluebirds, titmice. Banding carried on in the same locations gives data on the rise and fall over years of species, of range expansion and contraction. As our country homogenizes into suburbia the ground-feeding birds that eat injurious insects, the ground-nesting birds vulnerable to ever-increasing numbers of kids and cats and dogs and lawnmowers, are found annually in fewer numbers.

I used to make surveys along the Atlantic coast of the Least tern that fly north from South America to breed on our sand beaches and barrier islands. *This Thin Edge,* as Anne W. Simon terms it in her excellent small book on Coast and Man in Crisis, has been so overdeveloped, so overrun by vehicles, that our remnant colonies of terns, willets, plovers, pelican, and other sand-nesters must now be managed for survival, their breeding areas in many states posted and patrolled by concerned groups. On its South American wintering grounds the robin-sized Leasts—sea swallows—are killed for food, and for feathers (still) for Indian ceremonial robes. In California and New Jersey the Least has become a legally Endangered Species, as industry and housing contractors have found out to their enraged amazement.

In Massachusetts as I write this, the number of their colonies on the many-mile-wide beaches of the Cape Cod National Seashore has dropped from twelve (three years ago) to four, and the Seashore must employ wardens and student aides to protect this "national resource." At the critical period rangers lead fishermen's vehicles at night by flashlight, to prevent half-grown chicks from being run over in the beach buggy tracks where they sleep, or crouch at sign of danger. Like all teen-agers they like to wander. (Fishermen and rangers wander, too, but they aren't my job.) Kids and photographers throw rocks into colonies to make a cloud of birds rise and scream. Dogs run adult birds off their nests, leaving eggs and chicks vulnerable to sun, rain, and predators. I worked intensively on all this for ten years; you will have to put up with me. Never mind Arizona, this is more important.

In suburban woods, landowners fell dead trees because they look untidy, without regard for the nesting and winter refuges they provide, and the wildlife larders. It took years to persuade our Forest Service to leave pines for the Endangered Red-cockaded woodpecker, which depends upon diseased heart-wood for nesting cavities. How much do you know about food chains? How that swallowtail caterpillar chewing on your parsley today may tomorrow, via a careless young songbird that dined on it, be a hawk winging in airy grace over your meadow?

On the positive side, a woman who nurses injured Bald eagles for the Florida Audubon Society sat high in an eagle's nest for six days one recent June, to publicize the plight and hunting of our National Bird. Conservationists in osprey country erect old telephone poles with wagon wheels or cross-pieces on top, to encourage the nesting of this species, almost totally annihilated in the northeast by DDT, now making a comeback. (Note: Useful to the birds. A rim around the wagon wheel will keep nesting material from blowing away in winter storms, so that a pair returning next spring will find the old home right there.) In New Jersey where coastal trees are gone and telephone poles scarce, this species has opted for the girders of the power line towers that march across salt marshes to seaside communities. Hundreds of miles of Bluebird Trails are set out and maintained by birdwatchers, farmers, schoolchildren, senior citizens, garden clubs, retirees, in an attempt to keep these insect-eating and decorative members of our society alive and housed. If the houses are used instead by Tree swallows, do not be offended—Tree swallows eat enormous numbers of mosquitoes. If you must constantly evict startlings and house sparrows, clean the boxes, publicize their purpose, the effort is worth it.

Banding is involved in all these activities. As usual I have become deflected. I apologize for my digressions.

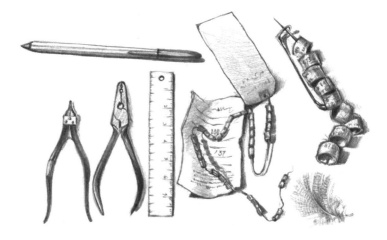

When I became a backyard bander I didn't know anything except to use care, and to learn the feel and structure and differences of the feathered fellow creatures I was studying. (I'm not sure I know much more now.) Using a special tool I open the individually numbered bands of designated sizes issued to me by our government, and close them, with a special tool, on birds' legs. So that if—IF—my victims are recovered dead or alive, their age, origin of banding, and migration paths are known. The percentage is very small. A bander in Tucson, Charles Cochran, has had only four of some 12,000 migrant White-crowned sparrows reported. White-crowns are small, inconspicuous birds, though, and there are few active banders in Arizona and northward. There are more in the East. My birds have been reported from Surinam to Ontario, each one a piece of information in the jigsaw puzzle—IF the finder reports date, locality, and band number to the U.S. Fish & Wildlife Service, Washington, D.C. (zip not necessary). You don't need to know the species; a computer will trace the number. Read that number carefully, though. Bands can be dirty and worn, and the lettering mighty small when seven digits have to fit on a ring around a wren's matchstick limb. The bands are made of an alloy, their weight is minuscule. People are always asking me about this weight, worrying. Does your wristwatch interfere with *your* balance and mobility?

Birds' legs don't change in circumference like ours. Chicks can be banded in the nest, early, before they flop out with the handling. But if you band nestlings a snake or a raccoon or other predator may follow your scent to a serendipitous supper, so I don't usually. A jay or a crow or a hawk, silent in trees above, may be watching. Some big birds eat eggs and little birds to survive. You eat eggs and chickens to survive, and find venison and duck more sporting than beef. Eighty percent of small songbirds will not make it through their first year anyway, what with weather, chancy food supplies, and predators (like cats). It is more productive to band them when they are on the wing. You learn things like this as you go along.

One thing I soon learned was that the Canadian Wildlife Service was far more rigorous—or impoverished—than ours. I banded mostly in our Canadian woods on Lake Erie in my early career; or on our beach, chasing the baby killdeer and Spotted sandpipers that very shortly could outrun me. An outmaneuvered sandpiper would run into the shallows, swimming under water with its tiny stubs of wings. I could catch them there, dry them, laugh at their long legs, and watch them scamper across the sand when released. Canada demanded not only a copy of the schedule sheets I must send to the U.S., but also a file card made out for each bird banded! Thank heaven we left Canada when my husband retired into government service and dragged me off to live in city hotels in foreign countries. Years later, in south Florida, as far from Canada as I could get, I might take 1,600 and more birds in fall migration alone. If I had had to fill out a file card for each one . . .

Widowed, I had parlayed my backyard fun into a serious avocation. I worked as a volunteer with the then only biologist at Everglades National Park, Dr. William B. Robertson, Jr., who knows more about southern Bald eagles and Sooty tern than anyone in the country. He dispatched me in the small Park plane to census the eagle nests and record their contents. Fresh linings? Eggs? Chicks? Fledglings? To take heron counts on the shallow Banks, and under the mangroves that edge the scores of small Keys dotting Florida's lovely translucent Bay. To photograph rookeries that from a distance looked like white chrysanthemum plants. To estimate for Audubon Christmas Counts the thousands of birds of a score of species in the ponds and sloughs and Bay and Banks—an impossible job, even for a professional. My pilot knew what we were doing, even if often I didn't. He became my landlord, letting me turn the land around a small cottage into a bird sanctuary. Together we flew low over the Everglades in flood and in drought, observing deer, shark, fires started by careless cigarettes, crocodiles, sometimes in the creeks even the shapeless blobs of manatees. (At least that's what Ralph claimed.) Herons and ibis streamed below us in clouds; snowdrifts of White pelican banked against the shores of inland lakes; coots stretched in solid rafts of thousands. In breeding season we flew in vertiginous circles to follow the feeding paths of Wood storks that in dry years might fly forty miles to obtain food for their young. I lived through a spell of dry winters, waking each morning to the smell of smoke in my nostrils, seeing my horizon murkily ringed from fires burning the Everglades to the north of me; driving the Tamiami Trail to Naples with flames crackling and blazing on either side of the road.

Sometimes on our flights we passed a peregrine (or it passed us). We flew, and at night to earn my pleasures, to thank Bill for this life he was giving me, I filed his data on the Dry Tortugas. I bounced, eager and enthusiastic, in and out of the Park offices. Everglades National Park was a small operation then. As it grew, professionals displaced my amateur efforts. Finally there were so many biologists they had to put up a separate building for them. I retired to my ten-acre sanctuary down a potholed lane so narrow that winter tourists hunting me had to leave their big cars out on the paved road and walk in (complaining) if they were to find the birds and me enjoying our seclusion.

Vacations, if you can consider the above "work," I went on exploratory bird tours to the Caribbean and Central America— five of us each winter with a venturesome and picturesque leader, C. V. Bowes, Jr. But I became tired of his showing me the hind end of birds I would never see again, whose names I could not remember, I wanted more productive occupation. So I deserted the cabin I had built in an Adirondacks hamlet to work one summer at the front desk of the Cornell Laboratory of Ornithology. Nights I labored on a translation of Maria Koepcke's book *Las Aves del Departamento de Lima, Peru.* I was house-sitting for Sewall Pettingill, Director of the Laboratory, and his beloved Eleanor (beloved by all of us) while he was off teaching in Michigan. I raised a baby Barn swallow on their dining table (sssssh) and was careful not to wind the grandfather's clock, which concealed their stash of liquor. Maria's small *Guide* is still the only one available for Peru. She had half completed a far more ambitious one when her plane crashed in the Peruvian jungle on Christmas Eve of 1971. Ten days later her sixteen-year-old daughter appeared down river at an Indian village, barely alive, the only survivor. The daughter made headlines. Properly; hers was an incredible survival. The loss of Maria, artist and scholar, went unnoticed except in the ornithological community. Worldwide.

At the Laboratory, against rules, I raised a kingfisher, robins, and other nondescript feathered—or unfeathered—small orphans that visitors dumped on my desk to the education and amusement of other visitors. The Laboratory was an educational facility, I excused myself defensively, founded to be a bridge between layman and professional. What should I do, toss these avian infants into the bushes? Instead I poked food into them every twenty minutes, sunrise to dark. Vitamins too. How did I know what their parents would feed them? Most hand-raised baby birds don't survive, or are released before they have learned to feed themselves. Some must be fed by the adults for weeks after they are out of the nest—look around your yard at those big, complaining beggars following and hollering at their harassed parents in early summer.

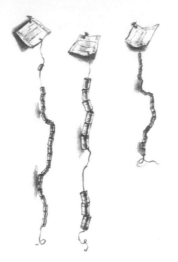

In Florida I started what became a ten-year migration study on my scrubby, overgrown, weedy, and wooded acres where a Green heron took up residence each summer in my absence and squawkily resented my returns. Dawn to dark each fall I ran twenty nets for the same six weeks in the same locations. Banding was not routine in those days, as recognized a tool as it is now. People came from all over the country, even from Europe, to see occasional rarities in the hand, and my wealth of Painted buntings. Two dozen of these brilliant beauties might be on my feeder at one time, often with vivid blue Indigos mixed in. The best viewing point was from my bathroom—a very small bathroom. I showed my slides of birds and their adaptations for living to thousands of schoolchildren and their elders, even once to a somewhat mystified but interested Chamber of Commerce, always making a pitch for conservation. I netted in an Ecuadorian rain forest with Bud Owre and his University of Miami students; in British Honduras-Belize with that country's energetic naturalist, Dora Weyer; in Trinidad and Tobago taking measurements for Richard ffrench, working on his excellent *Guide* to the birds of those islands. Yes, his name IS spelled that way, it goes back into the mists of Welsh history. Since he could not find an experienced secretary his wife Margaret learned to type and, slowly, patiently produced every one of those 740 invaluable pages.

In Trinidad I lived at Spring Hill Estate, a guest house in the Northern Range. Its redoubtable Icelandic mistress Asa Wright became a second mother to me, although she did NOT care for birds to be brought into her dining room, by me or even Maurice Broun, Director of the Hawk Mountain Preserve, and said so in stentorian tones. Don Eckleberry was working on his now famous tropical bird paintings there, setting the guests into gales of laughter with his stories, struggling to raise funds that would turn the Estate into a Nature Centre so it might survive Asa. (Surprisingly, he did.) At 4:00 A.M. I would be driven to the lowlands to set my nets; in hot noons run panting up from the rain forest, bringing him birds on his Want List until he begged me to desist, I was getting so many: some of them birds he had never hoped to study in the hand. He painted them, live, on his verandah while his wife, Ginny, fed them and I urged him to hurry, hurry, so they might be turned loose again. I had, as you can guess, a ball. All the time I was learning what I would need to know when I was on my own at Baboquivari. Asa even had peacocks. I never thought I would have to live with those honking, arrogant critters again.

My area in Florida changed, I had fewer birds. My friends moved or died or lived fifty miles away. To keep busy I wrestled the federal bureaucracy for a permit to band Brown pelican, an Endangered Species. Forms, forms, forms! If it weren't for connections in high places I wouldn't have that permit yet! It was required even just to transport injured pelican to the

veterinary center at the Miami Zoo, which I was frequently called upon to do. Illegally, Game and Fish men told me, when I was complaining how dangerous pelicans' panhandling is to the birds. I carried them with fish hooks caught in their pouches or bellies, feet sheared by boat propellers, stomachs fatally full of too-large bones thrown from fish-cleaning tables. As I drove the crowded six-lane highway into Miami on these thirty- or fifty-mile errands of mercy my efforts were compensated by disbelieving stares in traffic as one of my charges lifted its head to survey drivers on either side. I distributed thousands of SAVE THE BROWN PELICAN leaflets, warning fishermen and boaters.

"How do you transport these birds?" was one of the useless questions our government demanded an answer to. Out of patience with queries that in no way applied to my humanitarian efforts, I wrote on the form "in a whiskey carton" and heard no more. I *did* have to send them a picture of my aviary, which housed hawks, owls, baby mockingbirds, injured warblers, poisoned robins and flickers, once even an osprey whose cold stare and lethal talons terrified me, but never once did it hold a pelican! Permit finally in hand, I would drive down the

Keys, or to Flamingo, where pelican hang around marinas for handouts (and become injured). Swinging a mullet in my hand for bait, leaning off a dock or boat or ramp I would tease a bird close enough—with luck—to grab its bill, haul it in flapping, tuck it under my arm. Although an awkward handful, they weigh no more than a hen. I would inspect them for injuries, fish hooks, nylon line entangled in wing feathers that could—would—catch on mangrove branches at their roost and be their death. I would affix the large numbered band that years later is still being read by binoculars or telescope by visitors and reported. Pelicans are wary, though, hard to entice and bring within reach. All birds are smarter than Homo sapiens in his smug pride gives them credit for being. Once I had caught a couple of the young or greedy the rest would float in a group just out of range. As I swung my mullet forward they would rise, bills gaping, sink back. Like a ballet chorus. I might drive a hundred miles to take only three or four.

Marina owners often had a pet pelican that would come to their whistle for a mullet. (Mullets were free when I first did this. Later, with the decline of fish in Florida Bay, I might have to pay a dollar for one and was dismayed when a pelican, smarter than I, managed to pull it from my grasp.) Marina people never seemed surprised at my occupation, Florida is full of zanies. Bystanders were enthralled, so I did useful educational work for wildlife, explaining about banding, about migration (pelican migrate too), about the hazards these big birds face. I also contributed liberally to Kodak's coffers. I wonder how many photographs were taken of the rear end of this white-haired senior citizen in unbecoming postures, squatting, coaxing, lying on my tummy to reach off a dock, teetering on the rail of a boat? One day I lost a brand-new, expensive pair of sunglasses to a pelican. They were plastic and light, and its wing must have flicked them as I dropped him back into the bay. Vandalism? Petty larceny? Act of God? My insurance company never questioned, didn't even take their deduction. They wrote that they had never had such a claim, it was a pleasure to pay, might they use me in their newsletter?

Fishermen, although generous with heads and carcasses for bait, showed little interest. Occasionally I honey-tongued one into casting his line (after we had cut the sharp points off his lure) over a crippled bird. He would reel it in carefully, help me untangle yards of nylon line that might bind wings or neck, or force out a hook caught through the skin, or worry about sewing up a pouch. One day I saw my good friend Marge Brown, M. D., hook a pelican by accident, not knowing I was nearby. As I sprinted to her dock to help I heard her cry in desperation to her husband Harvey, also M. D., "If only Jonnie Fisk were here, *she* would know what to do!" What a rub on Aladdin's lamp . . .

Last year all those jillion robins didn't come as far south as Homestead. Too much food in the center of the state? I usually band five hundred of them in a couple of weeks around my pond, and later get some reported all the way to Toronto, Canada, as cats or cars or, more rarely, another banding station waylay them on migration. For the first time a pair of Sharpshins (a hawk species) were in my trees, interfering with my statistics as they snatched buntings off my feeders. Sharpshins have to eat, too, and are handsome raptors. They remove the incompetent or careless or ill from the population, so that only the smart and healthy live to breed. But of course once they find an easy source of food they settle in. Getting fat and lazy, which is bad for *their* population, and certainly for my disposition. I might catch one, transport it, it would swiftly return. Birds set up definite winter territories, just as they do summer feeding ones. Where I had had twenty birds at a time on a feeder, and visitors, I was getting only three or four of either. I told you that? Be patient. I promise you, we are practically in Arizona. You asked for this explanation, or if not you, half a dozen others. If I can get it down on paper I can forget it. It's my future I'm interested in, not my past. I was elected to Conservation boards, but I fall asleep in meetings. I am a field, not a policy person. I didn't have enough to do, I was restless. So I left Florida.

Banding is the common denominator of this long tale. It took me where I went, it got me here, writing by candlelight. Although—although—I have paused to pour a sherry. The night is wholly quiet, I am very alone. Thoughts I prefer to keep tamped down rise to trouble me. Is it really restlessness, the zest for adventure that has brought me to this cabin? Fear of the long gray winter months indoors on Cape Cod? Or, as ever, the loneliness?

I sweep uncomfortable questions under the rug. Gene's rug, a gesture of friendliness, a memory of merry Mexican evenings that is warming more than my feet as I sit at this black window. Probably I am just hungry.

What I am doing here for The Nature Conservancy (I begin tomorrow) is to document by netting, and banding with those small silver government bands, the birds on this high ranch. And, if I should encounter any, documenting the animals. Which I don't intend to net or band, just to eye respectfully from as much distance as I can arrange between us. The Conservancy gave me an award once. It was a Green Leaf pin, so tiny it became lost in a washing machine. They replaced it for me, and I lost that one, too. But I am on their books, I owe them my best service.

December 16th

A fine clear day; warm. Found a good bird lookout and a place to set nets on a nearby hill. Washed my hair. Walked the mile to Windmill Ford with Herman to investigate the bank at the former Creek crossing. I can slide up and down this on foot, but could never drive my car up it. Herman admits he had trouble, even in a jeep. He points out that the water level is falling. We pile rocks along the edge, trying to improve the situation, until I uncover *two* black widow spiders and decide this is a useless operation. Besides, I am hungry. Rancher Brother's son and a friend are here from the university to ride. Nice lads. Loaned me batteries for my tape player, explored my radio, worked on my corroded flashlight. They gave me the courage to light my propane lamp. At supper I contemplated that expensive pressure cooker I had bought, but put off using it. Wrote Christmas cards, drank a tot of Bud Owre's gift sherry, and was in bed by 10:00 P.M.

December 17th, Sunday

I wake to a gentle drizzle outside; inside, a drizzle onto the floor. The sink has again overflowed, water again runs along the shelves where my groceries live, I had better move them to those rickety shelves in the woodshed. Set these (groceries) under the stove, warm from last night's fire, bail (in reverse order), and run for Herman. The Peak is shrouded. Obviously with the Papago gods it is Out of Sight, Out of Mind, and I must care for myself. I stir up bran muffins and take them to the Big House. We sit over late Sunday coffee and I collect more stories—on riding fence, wetbacks (hungry but harmless, and we are far from the highway); dope smugglers flying over in unmarked planes. I am nervous about Bill's new Wagoneer being up mountain from the fords, but the lads assure me the rain is only a "soaker," to be expected this time of year, and a boon to ranchers. At noon they leave: they have a long drive ahead, and homework. Herman delays. He likes to redd up, put the chairs in alignment, wash his kitchen floor, sweep peacock droppings a last time from his porch. I return to my cabin, paperwork, and hot soup for lunch.

After a bit Herman knocks at the door, visibly distressed. It is raining hard. The Horse Bars Creek that runs down the gully—arroyo—by the Big House is swollen. He has been down to the Windmill Ford. The Creek is rushing, the bank too dangerously undercut to drive, he cannot leave. Little do we know it will be a good week before he can! This turns out to be our fringe of a One Hundred Year Rain that floods the whole Santa Cruz Valley, washing out bridges in Phoenix and Tucson and Nogales, homes and flood plains in its path, filling the DIPS DO NOT ENTER WHEN FLOODED with swirling streams for days, isolating whole communities. Later a postcard from Cape Cod queried me, WHAZZIT LIKE OUT THERE? I sent back a newspaper photograph of a whirlpool frothing around the top of a car that had skidded into one of those DIPS, with the laconic message "Sunny Arizona. Don't Come."

Herman spends the afternoon carrying in firewood from his porch. (My woodshed is sheltered and dry, full of apples and birdseed enjoyed by mice that slip under the door.) He alternates between sopping up leaks onto his floor and listening to weather reports. The peacocks huddle dismally under his porch roof, lined up on the benches. Banty stuffs birdseed with no competition, the rain sliding off his flaming feathers. The cats crouch on door sills out of the wet. They have given up trying to sneak in my door. I should be ashamed of my hard-heartedness.

Excited by this watery development in desert country I find my ankle-length slicker and slither down to Windmill Ford. Temperature moderate. Streams run across my route, a waterfall cascades over the bank at the exit. Haven't used my slicker in so long it leaks. Dripping, I report to Herman. What is one more puddle on his floor? Dripping, he later reports to me the news on the radio—all bad. In the early dark I write Christmas letters, although only the Papago gods know when they will reach a post office. Lamp light is hard on the eyes.

December 18th

Tucked down, relaxed and happy in my nest of blankets, I dreamed of Brad and his father, whom I also loved. The Indian gods are not the only ones watching over me from above. Slept again and woke to hard and ominous dripping. Mostly out-side, bless Herman and his tar bucket, but there are puddles in the bathroom and on my suitcases up under the roof. The cabin stands sturdily against heavy gusts of wind. Hindsight shouts that I should have taken Bill's Wagoneer across the fords yesterday when this "soaker" first started. Too late. I worry. To soothe myself I eat a huge breakfast of chicken liv-ers, toast, jam, and an orange the boys gave me. To Windmill Ford to admire the elements. Creek a roaring torrent, the road full of brooks to jump. Horse Bars Creek is a more challenging jump, but I do it. Was a broad jumper at Vassar.

December 19th. Gray

To the Ford again before breakfast. Cold—38 degrees at noon. Water abating, road drying. Herman on my roof again, trying to mend more leaks. Radio prediction of a possible thunder-storm, more rain, and *real* cold. We are stranded but cheerful. Chopped kindling, house-cleaned, dried things out. Wrote more letters. Have reached the bottom of my mail carton. First time in years.

December 20th. Clear

Cold in the night. Added a blanket and slept until eight. Am getting into terrible habits. Feel great. The Peak is rimmed with snow, jeweled edges sparkling in the sun. Did a laundry, mopped, cleaned the cabin, then went up Sparrow Hill with clippers and axe. Temperature 21 degrees at 7:00 A.M., Herman tells me.

December 21st

The Winter Solstice; the year's shortest day; the sun furthest south, its rays striking with a flat projectory, obviously having trouble getting over our hills

Light at 7:00, sun over the hill at 7:55, shining on my breakfast plate. Twenty degrees and clear. The stars last night were unbelievable. Kitts Peak Observatory is at the northern end of this mountain ridge. There is no light nearer than Tucson, if you except the small store at Three Points, to blur their and my heavens. I wonder if their scientists watched the stars in Capricorn change their course as our planet, last night, started to shift its tilt from dark to light under the arc of the sun? None too soon for me. What am I to do in this cabin, dark before 5:00 P.M.? The men were going to bring me up some research work from the university, but haven't yet. I now have twenty more pieces of mail to go out.

Am eating lavishly. So is a Hermit thrush, busy stripping the pyracantha bush outside my window. Pyracantha is not native to this altitude. Herman tells me Frances brought it here and he planted it for her by the doorstep. So she was lonely, too, remembering the plants of her home? Its berries must be a bonanza to a bird in this cold. They disappear though, too rapidly for just one customer, however hungry. (By the end of the winter I had caught ten thrushes. When the pyracantha gave out they entered my traps for grain. Didn't know they were seed-eaters.) They are birds of shrubbery, gentle, big-eyed, long-legged, slipping in when bigger birds are not about. I am partial to them from my memories of their sweet songs drifting down at dusk in Adirondack summers. I try putting out raisins for them, but the jays and thrashers gobble these up. At two dollars a pound I can't afford this.

Have I said that in the last three days we have had four and a half more inches of rain? I am supposed to record the weather, but I forget; it isn't yet a habit.

Morning:

Since my arrival December 12 I have observed twenty-four species of birds. I am waiting for the two ranch cats to be removed and for these unseasonal rains to cease before setting out my nets and going to work in earnest.

I wander about with binoculars and clippers deciding where to work. Tentatively I set up three nets on Sparrow Hill, with the thought that the cats won't prowl through the water of Horse Bars Creek to find them. I install a chair and my box of banding tools so I can sit, and guard against felines of any size. (I keep looking for the lion ones.) From here I have a sweeping view of the slopes, the Rhyolite Cliffs, the Peak, and birds flying back and forth. It is shirtsleeve weather this First Day of Winter, just what travel agents advertise for Arizona.

Afternoon:

I catch my first Arizona bird, a pyrrhuloxia. Pronounce it any way you want. These are regional differences in bird name pronunciation. I say *locksia,* out here they say *locksha.* By either one it is a finch, cousin to the cardinals, in the family of *Fringillidae,* the largest family of North American birds. That's the family that takes in grosbeaks, buntings, and those darned sparrows I don't know one from another. I better learn fast; there are plenty of them on these hills.

Birds don't have teeth. Seed-eating finches crack the tons of weed seeds they eat as a boon to gardeners with the edges of their bills. Cousin cardinal can raise a blood blister even on my tough hands. I was startled to see one fly like a flame across the Creek this morning. To me a cardinal is a dooryard bird, a southern species that around 1950 started to extend its range north. One of the first in Buffalo lived in our yard. That winter our young sons had no need to shovel a path through snow to our garage as so many birdwatchers came trampling in to admire this colorful rarity and add it to their lists. (From the breakfast table the boys would cheer them.) The species is now common in southern New England and still moving north. Bird feeding is done on such a large scale that recent harsh winters have not wiped them out. Although this may not be the reason for their expansion—who knows? In East Orleans on Cape Cod eighteen were reported at a feeder one wintry dusk. Mockingbirds and Carolina wrens and Tufted titmice also now winter north of former ranges, as do some orioles and chats that normally retreat to the tropics. All since 1950. Now we have learned that birds are valuable indicators of our environment we are paying attention to such changes. But seeing a cardinal at this altitude is a shocker. What next?

(Note: It never did tame and become a dooryard bird, although occasionally it took sunflower seed from my feeders. There was a pair. In the spring when they sang—the female sings almost as well as the male, one of the few species to do so—I could barely differentiate their song from that of the more common pyrrhuloxia. In fact, I never was sure. I found where they nested, though—deep in a thicket as they do in the East.)

December 22nd

Washed hair, pants, and self—Christmas is coming. I did a little banding; juncos and kinglets, a Chipping sparrow. Also a sparrow that isn't in guidebooks. (I have four.) An immature. It looks like a Cassin's, but no Cassin's should be here, not in this season. Damn, damn, they have sent a girl to do a man's job. Well, all I can report is what I see. I write a feather-by-feather description and photograph it seven ways to Sunday. Later the men identified it as a Rufous-crowned, common here. They had not seen it before in this plumage. The books show them only with rufous caps, which is what confused me. I took only one with such a cap, and that was in April when it had acquired its breeding plumage. A good bird identification guide needs paintings of a bird in both sexes and all plumages, which no one could afford to publish, or buy. Or carry into the field.

In the afterglow I made my daily run to the ford to listen for owls. There were none.

Letter to my sister, Winifred C. J. Chrisman

"Christmas! Whoever would expect Santa Claus to find me on this mountain, so far from anywhere? Nothing I can write could do justice to those two men in charge of me, and their wives. Santa is my host in Tucson, the one I wrote as a joke last summer about counting hummingbirds while I sat in a window doing needlepoint. There aren't any hummingbirds up here in winter, although in innocence I hung out a feeder of sugar syrup my first hour here. Aren't hummingbirds what all birders come to Arizona to see?

"In December, in subtropical Florida I would be planting snapdragons and green beans, picking oranges, living in shorts and feeding Florida hummingbirds. Here, after a week of waiting through dark cold days in Tucson I chivied Bill into bringing me up to this high canyon with its spectacular grassland slopes. (The prevalent cat's claw and the thorns on the mesquite don't show from a distance. You rode over this country, you know what it is like.) Bill HAD to bring me up, I was threatening to come back to you. That's what you get for giving such a fine Thanksgiving party. I've been making that hot spiced apple juice ever since—warm in my tum, and a wiser drink than rum when you live alone, stumbling around on a rocky mountain.

"We brought in the major necessities. The smaller ones, and comforts, I planned to get back in town a few days later. Hoho—there they are, here I am. I have chuckled at your letter indignantly informing me that it never rains in Arizona! A Hundred Year Rain flooded everything, ripped through highways and towns, rolled boulders into our fords, scoured out the creek beds we use as roads. All highways to the city were closed for days. I saw only our small part of it. It was exciting—water rushing down the arroyos, I could hear the rocks grinding even through my closed windows at night.

"I had made up my mind quite cheerfully, since I was personally warm and dry, to Spam and beans for Christmas dinner. I had a large woodpile complete with black widow spiders, a carton of mail, and paperwork to occupy me. Herman, the Ranch cowboy, was also beleaguered here, relaying news of the Outside World to me from his radio in the Big House. His batteries gave out after a while, but I had more. When the rain lets up he and the peacocks clamber about on my roof, trying to staunch the worst leaks, and thrash around in the brush fixing new breaks in our water system. Everywhere he goes the peacocks trail him. I was going to give out of eggs, but into every life some rain must fall, as Dad used to admonish us.

"Hacking a net lane through cat's claw after lunch I heard Bill Roe holler 'WHERE ARE YOU?'

"Company! I came running. In the yard, with their stout shoulders and sweating brows, were Santa Claus and his helper. Wide smiles, towering red packs, everything but white beards proclaimed CHRISTMAS. They were too laden even to be hugged. They escorted me to my cabin where the beer was and

ceremoniously, gleefully poured out on the rug the twin cornu-
copias of their packs. Gifts from all of you, in gay wrappings;
then oranges, grapefruit, apples, eggs, English muffins, Oregon pears Alice had wrapped, each one, in styrofoam against
bruising; rice, dried milk; peas and beans and prunes and apricots; fresh broccoli, bananas, thermal undies; books, a woollen
cap from my girl-Ranger tenants in Florida; rum, a chicken,
two Cornish hens (one for Christmas dinner, one for New
Year's); Amanda's annual, bulging, traditional Christmas
stocking topped by a snowman that I promptly hung on my
door. The men accepted beer and bananas and any sweets I
could find. What can you get for me to keep here for Bill? He
has a terrible sweet tooth, but doesn't eat chocolate. They
looked around, approved my improvements. Scott took a sparrow out of a net." (Note: that's how I found out what my
mystery birds were—Rufous-crowns.) "Then they set off down
canyon to go to a Christmas party of their own in Tucson. It
is a two and a half hour drive up here, and was two more miles
to pack all those gifts in. What am I doing for these blessed
people, how can I ever repay them? (Sweets! Please!)

"Just one Mexican bird," says Bill hopefully. I will have to
appeal to the Papago gods."

What a wonderful Christmas! No wonder I lost sight of the
factual calendar. Which I did, getting the rest of the week all
mixed up. Herman went out with the men, leaving his blue
jeep marooned here with their yellow one; there was no one to
straighten me out.

December 23rd. Morning

The jays have finally found the pottery feeder that young Rapp
Chrisman made me. It has a wide mouth that spills seed, to
the joy of the peacocks and Banty. Nets up all day, but only
ten birds banded—five species, though. The only one after
11:00 A.M. was a handsome, full-plumaged Audubon's Warbler in Christmas finery. The American Ornithologists' Union
now terms the Audubon's a "Yellow-rumped," lumping it with
the Myrtles. But since Magnolias, Cape Mays, and Yellows
also have yellow rumps I stick with the old name. So does the
Bird Banding Laboratory's computer that records our data.
Myrtles and Audubon's were lumped because in overlapping
territory they hybridize, but if I were to net an Audubon's in
Florida my yard would be full of eager listers from all over the
southeast. I don't know about Myrtles out here, if I get one
I'll find out. I would like a yard full of company.

By midmorning, once that fine golden globe that warms me

comes over the hills, my nets are in full sun, visible to sharp avian eyes, empty of birds.

Afternoon:

My Banding Office, up to now a chair-and-knee operation, I have formally installed on the sunporch of the Big House. This is a fine large room with plastic tacked outside its screens, set back from a cold north wind that has blown all this clear, 45-degree day. A shaky-legged big table holds notebooks and weighing scale, a smaller one my tools and clipboards. Bands hang in order on nails I hammered into railings. The light is excellent. A good place to work—sunny, sheltered, warm. Once I have totted up my morning's small catch of species—individuals, ages, sexes, fat deposits and all that—I bring up a deck chair, lunch and settle down with Edward Abbey's *The Journey Home;* then doze off, lulled by the Horse Bars brook running below me. When I come to—I must run the nets every half hour—the peacocks and Banty are all also snoozing as comfortably in the sunny flower beds outside, the tails of the peacocks shimmering in the sun. They haven't yet accepted me, their little heads move nervously when I move. Why are ranchers so fond of peacocks? Are they a status symbol, a fashion of twenty years ago that has hung on, surviving predators and isolation?

Inside the Office a dozen shabby, unloved plants trail dead leaves from old stools and makeshift tables, but trimming and some tender loving care can make them respectable. The room is hot as a greenhouse. When next I go to town I shall hunt up herbs and lettuces and pansies to decorate both diet and Office.

There is a skim of ice in a pail in the shade at 4:00 P.M., and I have worn long johns all day.

Evening:

It is easy to lose track of the days. I think this is Christmas Eve. I water the plants, I feed the peacocks a double ration, I tape Christmas cards to the door, inside and out, and move the little snowman with his shovel to the thermometer. The mice get extras in their traps, too, so they will die with full tummies. I light all seven candles, build a roaring fire (three sticks instead of two) in that stove, make biscuits in a frying pan to go under honey, and lentil soup for any visitors. I open the one can of frozen lemonade remaining for a special Father Fisk's Hot Toddy. We always left a mug of this in front of our Buffalo fireplace for Santa Claus. In the morning it would be gone. Hmmmm. Who was the last one stuffing the stockings? Or the first sleepy, curious child up? I clean my fingernails. A few presents I open, the rest I leave for tomorrow.

December 24th

Before I have finished my chores and can curl up with a second cup of coffee and the rest of my gifts two cold young mountain climbers down from the Peak knock at the door. They have been lost, spent an icy night roped to a tree on a narrow ledge, ran out of food. All I have hot and quick (they are in a hurry) is coffee and that pot of lentil soup, which they gratefully trade for the information that today is NOT Christmas. I have a whole, fine, extra day! I dish out more soup, and homemade bread. My social life, I have been told, will be the hikers and climbers to whom this Preserve gives access to the Peak, and they will always be cold and hungry. If I follow Frances's example (and look helpless) strong hands will open recalcitrant jars, cut branches from net lanes, and do other manly chores. Hikers are a special breed, never bums. (Note: I guess I don't look helpless. But all winter hikers took out mail, messages, and grocery orders, and gave me welcome company.)

Letter to the Spoffords

"I wish you could have been here when that Bill brought me Christmas, hiking in with Scott from below the second ford. (Bill's Wagoneer is stranded here until the Creek recedes.) What wonderful friends you produced for me! Those finger-free gloves from Eddie Bauer are a boon. I now also have thermal underwear, and a pair of lovely, soft, scarlet Pendleton slacks, just the garb for a country club New Year's Eve party with music, brandy, and champagne. "Sophisticated elegance," the tag reads, accurately. "To be brushed after each wearing." I had ordered them from the catalogue you sent because I need heavy warm work pants. All the Pendleton shirts I have owned have been rough and heavy, like Spoff's. Not even pockets in these lovely things! They are wrapped for return with a frosty letter inquiring as to whether Mr. Pendleton has grown so old and rich he has forgotten what camping is like

"I have two four-wheel drives standing in the yard. The near ford is impossible even to Herman the Cowboy. He went out with Bill to spend Christmas with his wife, like a proper husband. He likes it better here. The ford is a mile down Canyon. I walk to it every dusk, listening for owls I heard dueting the other night. Scott doubts they are sawwhets. My cabin is dark by 1700 and the litter on my table is discouraging, so I am glad to sally forth with a tape recorder and watch the stars come out. No luck on the owls so far. Yes, I DO carry a flashlight, stop worrying.

"I am writing this on my knee at my best birdwatching spot, guarding three nets I have set from the cats. There is little activity until the sun warms up insects, and by then the nets are wholly visible. I think of your home with all those different species coming to your dozens of feeders and am enormously jealous. The jays found my sunflower seed today, though; maybe they will toll someone else in.

"When you come up what I need is birdseed, suet, eggs, needles, yellow pads, magazines, a file box, and lots of disparate stuff. But since you are rumored to be extracting refrigerators and kitchen tables from the neighboring motel out of the trees after YOUR flood, I will probably get to Tucson—somehow—before you get here. Love and kisses and thanks for that handsome package Santa brought that doesn't rattle however much I shake it."

December 25th

I celebrate the actual day of Christmas by:

1. Sleeping until 8:30 in spite of the rooster crowing and the honking and foot-thumping of peacocks on my roof. No Donner and Blitzen they!

2. Donning red clothes, top to bottom.

3. Chewing down two Vitamin C tablets and throwing in an E for good measure.

4. Using the oven to warm the cabin instead of building a fire in the iron stove. The latter lasts longer, and takes no propane, but takes time to get going. Sun is streaming in the window and I plan to go exploring.

5 Hanging out my cosy cotton flannel sheets to air.

6. Giving the peacocks a double ration from the barrel in that old barn with such a spectacular view and sound of the Creek from its broken windows. I take special care to see that Banty and the half-sized hybrid get their share. They are outcasts from the more finely feathered flock, although I will take Banty's resplendent hot reds and oranges to the peacocks any time.

7. Sweeping my porch before breakfast. Well, I am outside anyway, reading the thermometers—42 degrees on the cheap one, 38 degrees on the better. And since sweeping is a frequent necessity due to that same feathered flock, I might as well do it now. Hoping Iitoi will look the other way politely— I am in my nightclothes.

8. Having for breakfast a cup of real coffee as opposed to instant; a perfectly boiled egg (accident); one of those delicious pears Alice wrapped so carefully; and my last two pieces of bread, so now I will HAVE to bake some. Toasted. By diligent search Alice found and sent up with Santa one of those old-fashioned slanting toasters built to set over a burner. Depending on the age and curvature of your slice part of it becomes healthily charcoaled; the rest is undamaged and lukewarm. I also scrape crystals from the frozen tangerine juice squeezed by me—all those bushels!—after we harvested the Roes' tree that midnight, and set them to melt in the sunny window. Alice generously sent this up; it is a celebration worthy of Christmas. That one sunny window, I should explain, is behind the stove, difficult to reach. No place for a chair there, to my regret.

I eat the pear from a plate with a chickadee on it, given me for Christmas one winter when feeding chickadees off my fingers was a specialty I showed off to our city friends. I eat my egg from a plate with a pelican on it—a gift I unwrapped last night from Ann Gaylord, who had whooped and hollered watching me try to catch pelicans. That very hard-to-get federal permit to band pelicans is in my luggage, but not much use to me here. I am a long way from Florida Bay.

9. Reading a chapter in a Christmas gift book.
Let us take these various holiday celebrations in order.

1. In ordinary living, in other climes, I am up and doing anywhere from 5:00–6:30. Sleeping until eight indicates serious illness. But here it is dark. Snug beneath a mountain of blankets, by turning my head I can see light slowly diffuse through the tangled branches of that mesquite where last week I had watched the moon set. It is all right for me to be slothful—it is too cold to open nets, quite aside from being Christmas, when all God's creatures should go unmolested. Not cold for me—I can start my days with long johns and heavy jackets and a beret and gloves—but for the birds. If they are flying at all in this dusky hour they need every scrap of energy to sustain their fragile lives. I except Mexican jays. These critters must be able to live through anything with their strong crankiness undamaged. By 9:30 on usual days, the sun warming my land, I have come in, undressed, and started over again with only normal coverage. 2, 4, 8, and 9 are self-explanatory.

3. Health addict friends in Florida pressed on me Vitamin C for colds and general well-being, Vitamin E to rub on wounds and absorb in great quantities for rattlesnake bites. This latter may become necessary when these reptiles emerge from hibernation. Herman has warned me to keep my screen door securely closed—Frances had rattlers come inside, seeking warmth. At the moment there is definitely no warmth to my cement floor, and if I leave the door ajar what I get are cats and peacocks. I don't know what the bottle of multiple vitamins is for but take one once in a while on general principles. My diet is not the best because I am lazy and there is no one to chivy me.

5. How do you wash queen-size flannelette sheets in a sink too small for a skillet? In the bathtub is the answer, the water trickling in slowly. What a chore. Another day, not Christmas. I had expected to use laundromats in town (seventy-five

miles), and to purchase a second set. I didn't figure on RAIN.

I reheat the coffee and set about opening the lumpy red flannel Christmas stocking that every year, no matter where I am, our beloved daughter Amanda manages to get to me.

Footnote. The mice ate every scrap of the Christmas dinner I set out for them, and left not so much as a whisker to thank me.

Still Christmas. Midmorning:

I pack a sandwich and start on a Christmas Explore. The trail
up mountain lures me, but I go down canyon in case Bill really
meant that he and Alice might come camping. I hardly imagine that with two small children, a host of relatives and friends,
they will show on Christmas Day, and I have told them over
and over that they are not to worry about me, but just in case
. . . Bill is an unpredictable fellow, always reaching for more
than his grasp and usually getting it. Maybe he likes to go
camping on Christmas. I love to see his cheery face approaching, and to watch him hunt along my shelf for a sweet.

I wear my red jacket and beret so the mountain lions will
know it is Christmas. I need to see if the Creek has abated
enough at the first ford for me to cross it on foot. If so, I will
proceed to the second ford and judge my chances of driving
my car across it. If so, then I can bring my car up to the
windmill and pack my supplies in only one mile instead of
two. Hurrah!

I saunter along in holiday leisure. The foothills open out,
disclosing, far down, the floor of the desert and the distant
range of the Atacoscas. Sometimes this range shows sharp and
clear, sometimes blue with haze; in the late afternoons shad-

owed and purple. I've been told their soft haze, depending on the wind, is smog from the copper mines. I don't know. When Altar Valley is cloud-filled the opening stretches gray-blue and infinite. Like the Atlantic I trudged those many years, hunting tern colonies. I said this before, why can't I say it again, it's Christmas?

I pick up rocks from the crown of the "road" and pile them in gullies that cross it. This is, I tell myself, so I won't stumble on them in the early starlight, listening for owls, but really it is the damming instinct in every healthy Outdoor American, reaching its flower in the Army Corps of Engineers.

The Creek has narrowed but still runs swiftly. Basic rock colors the water a clear and lovely green, smooth as jello. I am amazed that Rancher can jounce over this, but his truck sits high, probably he can do it in the dark. A polio hip makes walking difficult for him. I scrabble along the edge and find a spot shallow enough to jump and splash across. Deer tracks show in the sand, and two sets of animal tracks, smaller. Skunk? Hare? I wade on and come out by the windmill and a cattle tank. Near them, sheltered by trees, are the remains of an adobe hut. Until last winter this was in good condition, Herman told me angrily. It offered shelter to campers and wetbacks, delight to artists and photographers. Beer-happy young people or hunters—they have left their spoor behind them—senselessly knocked all but one wall down. I speculate on who may once have lived here, miles in from the road to Mexico.

Beyond the windmill the way becomes really rugged, with outcrops no bulldozer could remove, they will need dynamite. The road twists uphill and down, fissures tilt this way and that, there are abundant small gravelly streams and gullies. I see tire marks—yesterday's lads?—and the footprints, dried in the dirt, of Santa Claus and his helper. So they had had to stop down at ford 2—a long uphill way to carry those gift-laden packs.

The land becomes gentler, thick with ocotillo. "Thick" means these graceful bushes grow fifty to one hundred feet apart, their roots seeking water. In a few months the thorny, whiplike stems should be fountains of red on the slopes. I muse on photographs I will take. Now the hills are opening wide, I can see the desert stretching brown, mile on mile. The day has grown warmer, and sunny. I had considered wearing for this holiday jaunt the gay straw hat I bought in the Bahamas last winter but had opted for my Christmas-red beret instead. A mistake. I hang my jacket on a bush to retrieve on the homeward path. I ignore the fact that I am walking mostly downhill, and that what goes down must come up.

Ford 2 is at the confluence of two creeks, one broad, one swift and narrow. A creek in Arizona might be called a river in other places (have you seen parts of the Rio Grande?), a brook, or a stream or kill. By any name these two are wet and present difficulties. Where the road crossed last year is now a jumble of tree trunks, brush, and boulders. Rancher has carved a new passage. It enters over rocks, runs along the creekbed, turns aside for the largest boulders, exits on a sharp angle through soft gravel where tracks show someone has been in trouble. Hmmm, *I* should attempt this?

Up the steep hill just beyond, under its thorn tree sits my VW. Safe. Washed clean. Unless we have a dry winter, unless the road repair is more effective than I suspect, this is where my personal transportation will halt. Two miles, reads the gauge on my hip. Easy downhill, not so easy going up, tugging supplies. I cup my hands in the clear water of the Creek and drink. Rancher allows fifteen acres to a cow, I am not too afraid of contamination. And I am not the only one to drink here. In the damp sand are more deer prints and two sets of cat's paws, one large, one small. Bobcat? Mountain lion? A lion and her cub? Rancher will be interested in this. I need a pocket rule.

"Unless you've measured it, you don't know what your're talking about" (Lord Kelvin, *Primer of Population Biology*).

What tag ends from our teaching linger in our minds! Have you ever measured a bird's egg? You don't do it casually, by thumb or ruler, you use a special caliper. If you are careful and quick the parents won't mind, or even notice when she—or he—returns that you have crayoned a date on it to time its incubation period. I need that caliper here for footprints. Or plaster of Paris. Well, today my fingers will have to do.

The way back seems shorter. Sparkling with icy jewels for the holiday, Baboquivari rears against the blue sky. I break stride twice, once to sit in the shelter of mesquite by a purling brook and nibble on nuts and apricots. A hawk speeds low over a hill and is gone behind me, doubtless seeking its own Christmas nuts and apricots. Once to study a mixed flock of birds conveniently feeding on the roadside. I hold up binoculars until my arms ache, trying to identify a woodpecker that in the fashion of birds stays on the far side of branches. The sparrows and towhees are more friendly. Sparrows are nondescript streaked little brown birds. Even in the hand, bird guides spread open before me, their streaks, collars, whisker marks, bars, and bill colors are difficult to key out. In the field now you see them, now they dive into a clump of grass or walk behind a bush and you don't. I am no one to call their names.

The sun is sliding down over the ridges as I reach the home stretch and fasten the gate that proclaims PROPERTY OF THE NATURE CONSERVANCY. Not yet used to the altitude and the hiking, I am weary. I may be able to pack in Kleenex and paper towels and thread and suet and hamburger, but not the

card table, file cabinet, fifty pounds of birdseed, dishes, canned tomatoes, and other assorted needs.

Back in the cabin I rummage in the Christmas sock for a chocolate bar and make cold tea. No need for ice—the water comes straight from those jewels on Baboquivari. I scatter grain for the peacocks.

Other times, other places, at Christmas twilight it would be eggnog or champagne in a crush of partying friends. And later, the partying, the visit to grandparents over, hot soup for the children and a quiet cup in the warmth of home with Brad. But I am content. That past has been blocked off by many gray and lonely years. I have built a new life, useful, with new friends. And if I do not recognize the woman I have become, if sometimes I yearn desperately for those former days, it does not really matter. Santa Claus still has found me; the gods of Baboquivari have me in their hands. I light my lamp and select a book.

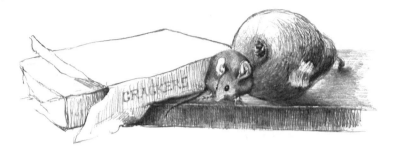

December 26th

The face of Baboquivari is brightening at 6:50. At 6:58 the first peacock thumps on the roof and pads about, followed by his friends. At 7:02 Banty crows, first in the distance, then closer. I set nets before breakfast to see if birds are flying, and bait traps on Sparrow Hill. By 9:00 I have caught nothing. I slept poorly last night. (I'm not used to all this sleep, it's getting me down.) About two o'clock I heard a click, and then odd noises. My flashlight showed the second mouse of the night caught by a leg in the trap, still stuffing itself on a peanut. I hate to kill creatures, but I had to. In this cabin it is the mice or me. You'd think those damned cats would keep them under control, but they are too busy ambushing Brown towhees.

I pour another cup of coffee to pass the time. I leaf through a slim volume eight-year-old Barbara Ann Roe has sent up for me to share—*Prayers from the Ark*. Lovely illustrations. Rumer Godden found these poems when she was helping some nuns clean a cupboard in a London convent. She translated them from the French with love and sensitivity. My eye stops at "The Prayer of the Mouse."

> I am so little and grey,
> dear God,
> how can You keep me in mind?
> Always spied upon,
> always chased.
> Nobody ever gives me anything.

What a false complaint! Who spies on whom in this cabin, I'd like to know, skittering behind the plates on that shelf? The French are thrifty, must be more careful with their foodstuffs than I (maybe they have more tin boxes). Crackers those mice get from me; apples; pounds of sunflower seed—there is always a trail of shells coming from under the woodshed door. Who is it has thieved the insulation from my fridge, who investigates my warmest socks? Don't tell *me*, little friends, that you "nibble meagrely at life!"

I muse on this Frenchwoman with the international name, Carmen Bernos de Gasztold, whose life had been so full of terror and difficulties; on how she came to rest at last, writing in what had once been the *columbier* of an Abbaye south of Paris. What rustles did she hear at dusk, living high in her dove house, what beating of wings in the night?

Letter to a good friend and eminent scientist

Ten days ago he had written me one of those $7.50 Deliver Today letters, asking if he might come to recover from asthma in the clear dry air of Arizona. Bill had brought the letter when he came up with Christmas. In the

*bleak weather of that week before Christmas I might as well have been liv-
ing in dour Boston, where Ian lives.*

"The reason I didn't encourage Bill Roe to encourage you
to come is that I don't really have my feet under me yet. While
the surroundings are magnificent, living isn't easy. I've camped
little, and then Brad handled it. I've never tented, as you do
summers; my standards are different. It is COLD until the sun
comes over the ridges (if it does at all) at 8:00 A.M., and often
again by 3:30 or 4:00 in the afternoon. I find cooking by
flashlight unsatisfactory, never was a Julia Child. My one table
is piled with papers, which I push aside to find room for a
plate and mug. (I have two of each, though.) Everything in
the fridge is frozen solid but the eggs. Mice have removed the
insulation, so even Julia might have troubles. The one lamp
lights only the table. There is a big, drafty ranch house (which
leaks) where you could stay, but the Ranchers have leased it
back and come occasional weekends, I never know when.

"When the weather warms—February? March? your sons'
vacation?—you and Shirley might very much enjoy camping,
as you suggest. There are trails to an incredible peak that looms
over the Ranch. The boys can climb in all directions, break
their necks, get lost, have a fine time. As I hope Bill warned
you when he telephoned, he would have to drive you seventy
miles to where you pack in, due to washouts from our recent
Hundred Year Rain, just after our Hundred Year Freeze. Did
he also tell you the Spoffords lost their pumphouse at Cave
Creek Canyon, but acquired furniture from the motel just
beyond them? In their trees! The new owners are Easterners,
who didn't believe warnings about flash floods and built a new
unit down by the summer brook because it was so pretty there.

"I am writing this on my knee at 38 degrees, net-sitting at

93

what I hoped would be a safe distance from a flock of peacocks
and a love-starved huge black ranch cat, but isn't. There is a
second cat. Rancher promised to remove them but hasn't. And
now that they would have to be packed out two miles in cages
I fear he never will. Even he couldn't get his truck up here the
last time he tried.

"You push yourself so hard I am not surprised your system
rebels. Of course you are welcome, and by all means come,
but when you can get here more easily. The road is to be
scraped and repaired "next year." After the ·hunting season.
January? February? When the weather is more clement. The
spring flowers should be a Hundred Year Wonder and entrance
Shirley and her paint boxes."

I opened nets for an hour, but it is too cold to let birds hang
in nets. At noon Rancher and Son barrel through Horse Bars
Creek in their ancient truck. To check on me, and to do a few
chores. I have been worrying and worrying about Bill's Wagoneer, sitting up here because of his generous gesture, when I
know he needs it for the Christmas counts he leads. Rancher's
Son offers to drive it to the highway for me. I scrabble together
overnight needs and we take off. Slowly. As Rancher negoti-
ates the first ford he admits there are boulders where he least
needs them. At the highway he gives me my second lesson in
four-wheel driving, and turns south. I travel north, gingerly
at first, then with confidence; it is an easy machine to handle.
I stop on the outskirts of Tucson for a poor hamburger, become
confused on the crisscrossing highways, and shortly find myself
lost in a city I don't know, in the dark, in an expensive new
vehicle that doesn't belong to me and that I don't want to
crump. The streets have familiar names but end in railroad
yards and industrial dead ends.

When finally I pull into the Roes' driveway I am tense, tired, and woebegone. The door has double locks, and my fingers are cold. Two slavering Boxers wait, snarling, for me. (Once I am inside they are lap-sitters and chocolate bar thieves.) Alice hears my fumbling with the key. Her expression registers more than just surprise.

"Delivering a car," I mumble. "Knew Bill had an Audubon Christmas Count tomorrow. Thought he would need it."

Bill, as always, is on the phone. Its long cord trailing, he paces into the hall. His eyebrows shoot up, too. I am welcome but there seems to be a problem.

They burst out laughing. "Guess who is in your bed?"

A head pokes around the corner. Here in my hand is my letter to my friend Ian saying *Don't come*. There in the hallway, in pajamas, is my friend Ian, looking frail, looking tired. Quickly I shove his letter into a pocket.

Alice never flaps. While Bill builds me a hot rum, because he thinks my delivery deserves a celebration, because I think I need something to restore my wasted tissues after the strain of getting his vehicle here intact, because it is the day after Christmas, she disappears. I have met several pleasant men in Tucson, but my real boy friend is three-year-old Henry Roe. Alice is making up a bed in his room for me. Henry is delighted. I am delighted, even at five the next morning when he feels he has to show me all his presents. I can't understand the words that tumble out in his eager, shining-eyed enthusiasm (Alice often can't either) but love has few restrictions, and we get along fine. Henry running to hug me on arrival, tugging at my hand to share some treasure, inviting me—always—to share his room again, is one of my winter's happiest memories.

December 27th

Off early to market for supplies. Then the Roes and I, Ian, guests, and a picnic lunch fit into our two vehicles and drive up to the mountain. We stash the VW again under its thorn tree. It may be vandalized sooner or later, but probably not, they say cheerfully. In case of more rain—a ridiculous notion at this time of year in Arizona—I can safely drive out from here, give or take a flooded sandy wash. Two runs in the Wagoneer get us and my supplies to the Ranch.

"You see?" Bill says, inspecting Herman's neat blue jeep, still in the yard. "You had *two* four-wheel drives at your disposal all through the bad weather. Didn't you feel comfortable?" I snort.

The children splash in a pond in Horse Bars Creek, now a

manageable brook. Their elders hike, walk around in the sun, sit on rocks. I stow away supplies. Herman installs Ian in the one bedroom in the Big House that doesn't leak, but does have the Canyon wren hopping sociably in and out through some small opening. Herman stays the night, checking woodpiles, tarring the roof again. Rancher had brought him up, taking away in exchange the big black cat. This leaves only Pinto, a mighty hunter who lives off the land, for me to worry about. A fluttering bird in net or trap is bait to any cat.

Alice had found me a sturdy card table. Ian and I set it up in the center of the cabin. Never mind having to pull in my tummy so hard to skirt it; the next week we live at it. Immediately after the others leave the weather turns as chilly and wet as New England in late December. Clouds are dank over Baboquivari and the Rhyolite Cliffs. We sleep late—just what Ian needs. He makes bread and delicious tidbits out of what he has brought from a Boston health food store. We set out traps where we can watch them from a window, gleefully attracting a few jays and a Brown towhee. We open nets on Sparrow Hill and set up a new one for juncos by the barn where the peacocks feed. Since there are two of us to run back and forth, against common sense we erect two more in the wash beyond Sparrow Hill, under oak trees. Only last week a shallow river ran here. Deer and horses run here too, I worry. Herman leaves. Ian clears space for yet another net in the cat's claw and burry weeds and vines of my back yard. The peacocks observe this—is there anything they don't?—and shortly fly through it. I finish the supplementary clipping and raking—woman's work—as the rain starts. A drizzle. We decide this is a gentle rain, a ground-soaker, but to be on the safe side we furl all nets tightly and go inside to light candles and concoct supper.

December 28th. 2:00 A.M.

In the night a spatter of rain on the roof, a trickle dropping from the eaves onto the trash can that holds birdseed, pulls me partly from sleep. Drowsing, I am back on that sea and sunswept island in the British Virgins where Brad and I used briefly to escape the rigors of Buffalo winters and his department store stress. Just so rain would run across our roof in the nights, trickling tinnily into a cistern. Warm in love and content we would listen to the sea surge on the cliff below us, the rain skitter swiftly, then cease.

But this rain does not cease. It drums on the roof, slaps the window by my head, streams noisily now onto that trash can. I come fully awake. This is not Guana Island but a desert mountain 2,000 miles away. I am alone, there is no competent, comforting man to handle my responsibilities.

I think. My car is OK, it is on high land. The leak talking in the kitchen needs only a bucket under it. Ian is on his own there in the Big House—probably too conked out in his fatigue to know it is raining (or else dreaming he is back in Boston). I have extra nets but my poles are precious—aluminum, light, jointed, especially made for me in Homestead, Florida. Far away. Water flooding the wash may carry them downstream and damage them on rocks. I pull on slacks and a sweater and sneakers and the slicker I have worn more in two weeks in the Sun Belt than in two years in the East, and hope the batteries of my small flashlight are good. I sent Ian off to bed with the big one.

I slog out. Horse Bars Creek has risen, the road up Sparrow Hill runs water. In the dark all dreads are worse. Rain from the Rhyolite Cliffs cuts a new channel beside the poles in the gravelly wash. I gather in the nets, anchor the poles up the bank in shrubbery. For good measure I also take down one in a gully still dry, then slip and slosh back to shelter and a hot bath. If you can call two inches of lukewarm water that. And return to my fine warm nest of blankets.

December 28th

Letter to the Lime King and Orchid Queen of Florida, Liz and Harold Kendall. Liz had promised to come to call, even if she must do it on mule-back. She never made it. I heard about her living the soft life in California.

"My gauge has now registered over six inches of rain since I have been on this mountain in the Sun Belt Liz remembers so fondly, and I have been three times isolated beyond impassable fords. Fortunately I had food, firewood, and mail enough to keep me for months. I have three chairs, an adequate john and a bathtub (the latter too chilly nights and dawns for use), nine peacocks, a Bantam rooster, a cat. What more does Liz want? The hills are full of mule feed.

"So far someone has managed to get here once or even twice a week to check on me (tenderfoot). I missed your Christmas Party. Thought of you with all those grandchildren so formally dressed, racketing on their miniature train through your avocado groves, probably snatching your prize-winning orchids off the trees; crawling between the guests' skirts by the tree. Next year. . . . Christmas here was—well, different. Not exactly traditional!

"We have been wrapped in cottonwool cloud all week. Clear

nights are marvelously beautiful, the stars are poetry. I am learning to cope. The birds mostly are new to me so I do a lot of plumage study.

"Small world! Your California hostess used to live on a ranch just down Altar Valley from here. I chuckled over you both being caught trespassing in my sister's garden, which has been pictured more than once in *Sunset* magazine. I wouldn't dare pick even a pansy there.

"Tell those fishing Dr. Browns we just ate a supper of the canned mussels they gave me. Surprise for my guest, who expected western beef! He will mail this when he goes out.

"If Liz still plans to visit on muleback she should pack ponchos, rain gear, and lots of sweaters. "BE PREPARED," I write the college kids asking to come up on vacation and Share My Fun. "Carry a shovel and peanut butter in your car." They are welcome—not on my terms but on those of the terrain. By the time my answers reach them they are back in school."

New Year's Day

I hadn't expected to live this long. Years ago I decided that
sixty was old enough, but I have gone on and on and on. And
here I still am, cosy under my covers, listening to wind rattle
branches against the roof and peacocks rattle their feet ditto,
with another New Year ahead of me. The sky is clear, sunlight
is yellow on the Peak. I get up, shovel out the ashes from last
night's fire. We sat long over a feast of Cornish hens, spaghetti
squash, fruit cake, wine and coffee and candlelight.

I go outside for kindling. A skim of ice is on the peacock
pans. Minimum temperature in the night registered 20 degrees,
now at 7:30 it is 34 degrees. I fill the coffee pot to the brim,
bring out sausage and eggs and the bread Ian kneaded to while
away yesterday's rain, set the bones from those delicious hens
to simmer for soup, fix my last grapefruit to celebrate New
Year's Day. I hope I won't be present another year, but you
never know. After Brad died I passionately wished each night
for years that I might wake up dead in the morning, but I
haven't. I suppose I have led a useful life in these seventeen
years, once I got hold of myself, once Bill Robertson and Matt
Baird pulled me out of those dark caves I hid in. Gradually I

built a new life around field ornithology and working with young biologists. I don't regret those years now, but I want life on my own terms. When I can no longer be independent I hope I have the guts to quit.

Well, there is my New Year's wish. And here comes my guest, bundled to the ears. He went for an early hike and is hungry.

January 4th

Perihelion—the day that our planet is closest to the sun. Only it must be some other section of our planet than S. W. Arizona.

I have been Outside for two days. I picked up mail, had my car serviced, washed my hair and those flannelette sheets, reported to my sponsors, comforted small Henry when he fell out of bed at 4:00 A. M., ate a proper piece of toast, and shopped for those little needs a woman finds necessary—oilcloth and postal cards, cuphooks and nails and—too late for Ian—dinner plates; more pads of paper and pens and stamps and a Timex with a second hand to replace the one the mice have stolen; a secondhand chair to replace the one with a broken leg; extra car keys; apples, bananas, lettuce; a quart of real milk, even if I must suffer the weight of this latter in my bulging pack.

Leaving the city I congratulate myself that for once I have managed to get Everything. I always leave something behind, but this time NO. (And where is my warm red Vyella shirt, hmmmmm? Back in Alice's guest room.) I stop at a nursery to see if they have parsley plants. No, so I buy lettuce seed, it will grow quickly on that sheltered sun-and-work porch screened from peacocks. For soil there is plenty of old chicken manure. Gardening makes me think of a shovel—mine lives in the back of my car. I pause. It, and my ten-dollar chair and the carton of essential propane cylinders for my lamp are back in Tucson, at the door of the Roe's garage. Damn and double damn. I am such a cluck!

I go back. Not wanting the Roes to learn I am so stupid I park on a side street, sneak down their back alley, load, and hurry away. You can't keep a secret in this world. Along the sidewalk skips six-year-old Barbara Anne Roe. She waves madly as she recognizes me, is hurt that I don't stop, and of course will tell her mother . . .

Traffic is backed up for street repair. Behind me a man runs into a new Chevrolet and rams it into my bumper. The girl driver cries. We exchange names (I am undamaged) and I hurry away. Leaving the Scene of an Accident I worry. Never mind, it is late, and I must drive fast. The sun sets early in January, earlier still in my foothills; I must be home before dark. The fissures and rocks of my private eight-mile entrance are frightening enough without being exaggerated by shadows. I munch on my twelve o'clock peanut butter and jelly sandwich at four.

As I open the cattle gate off the highway I realize that for the first time I am driving up to the Ranch alone. No one expects me back in town for three weeks. If I snag on a rock, slide into a gully, no one will come looking for me. There is no one within miles to help me. A sobering thought. I drive through a broad gravel bed, with water still running, where Ian had had to shovel a rock base on our way out. I manage the two narrow dips where it is easy to leave a tailpipe. I come to a ford I don't recognize, but I must have crossed it successfully two days ago, so I grit my teeth and Go. I come to another I want no part of and get out and study it and get in and Go. I see an abandoned car part along the road, but am too busy twisting a way up a hill to identify it. I wind my way between and over boulders, pass by mistake my parking slot, back in haste from the declivity leading down to Ford 2. OOOOOF, I have made it. Looking up at the Peak, I thank Iitoi.

Now for the footwork. I eat an apple for strength. My niece gave me a small daypack as a joke last summer—just the right size for my aged years. I swing it on my back, hang my binoculars around my neck, shoulder that clumsy but useful National Audubon Society pack I once bought at a Board Meeting, hide my car keys under a rock for Rancher to find, and start The Long Trudge. When Rancher or Herman come they will pick up my larger purchases.

I wade the creeks, picking shallow places, stopping often to puff and admire the views. Where the hills block the sounds of the Creek I am aware of my heart beating woodenly.

"Take these long hills slowly," Rancher has warned me.

The packs grow heavier. That quart of real milk, the can of bacon, the lettuce I couldn't resist, the mail . . . although some of this should be compensated for by the dirt the dry cleaning establishment removed from my woollens.

Here and there I can still see Santa's footprints. I think of him, and our daughter, and all the city people at this hour—feeding children, turning on TV for the evening news of riots and fires and wars and politicians, the marvelous sky of dusk blocked from their view by roofs and walls. As I unlock the final gate the last light is reflecting off the Rhyolite Cliffs. I wish on the first star. There is no sound—no ambulance or police siren, no owl, no wind. The stream at the horse bars runs its music. By the light of a quarter moon I fumble on the nail for the house key, scatter grain for the peacocks to find in the morning, and bring in my laundry. The traps have each caught a mouse to put in Pinto's dish. The pilot of the fridge has blown out again. Ian must have left the good flashlight in the Big House, I can't find it. I am home. From the black mass of the Peak the gods look down on me.

January 5th

When I went out last night to say goodnight to the moon and the Milky Way the sky was covered with round white cloud pancakes. Like snow patches on black ice, only overhead instead of underfoot. Or was this a mackerel sky, like those of the East, pressing low on this high land? This morning Baboquivari's stony bulk looms hostile and colorless. In the east clouds are massed over the valley. I hurry breakfast, wanting those cuphooks and fresh vegetables from the car before the creeks run high again. The University packed me a box of specimens (dead birds, skinned and stuffed with cotton): I need these to study sparrows. Sparrows are stripy little brown birds that mostly run on the ground behind clumps of grass and bushes. I said this before, I can't say it too often. Even in the hand their differences are subtle ones—horizontal, inconspicuous feathers denoting one species, vertical another; a rufous shoulder that doesn't show when a wing is folded; prominent markings on an adult male not prominent at all, or missing, from the female or immature bird. If it is going to rain again, these specimens will occupy me.

By the time I reach the car the sky is brilliant, the sun hot. I peel off two layers. Old Babo has resumed his purple and chartreuse. I stuff my sack—those good apples, they will fit in, too—and cross the first Creek on stepping stones I have placed for this purpose. Water flows over them and they turn under my feet, but I am careful. I idle, sketching the animal tracks I find. Rancher tells me what they are. I *must* remember to carry a ruler. Again I drink from my hand. Edward Abbey stresses the dangers of dehydration in this country, leading to kidney stones. He warns against minerals in the water, too, trying to keep too many people from infesting his beloved desert. I disregard the minerals; I am always thirsty.

I find fresh scat, full of fur. Is there a book on animal scat? I need one. Few birds are along my way, or perhaps I do not notice them, having to watch where I set my feet. If I don't, rocks trip me and I skid on loose gravel. Quail talk from the hillsides, jays and flickers and an occasional hawk fly in sight long enough to recognize, but those little birds—sparrows!— darting into oaks, scuttling in grass, are too swift to distinguish. I am not a good field ornithologist. Maybe these bird skins I carry so carefully will help me improve. I idle again at the second crossing, building a dam in the shallow rapids, playing, getting hungry. Getting chilly. Clouds like dark smoke are blowing past the mountain's face. By the time I am inside and have eaten lunch it is raining hard.

Spent the afternoon screwing in cuphooks, tacking oilcloth, mending a chair, hiding cereals in tins against the mice. Made a suet feeder, although the birds here certainly don't understand handouts. There is not enough birding to make an honest woman of me.

January 6th

An inch of rain at night, intermittent during the day. Abbey writes of a fire lookout whose laconic, obligatory diary read, day after day—"Done my usual chores." A useful phrase. I done my indoor ones. *The Journey Home,* Edward Abbey, E. P. Dutton, $4.95 paperback and worth every penny whether you are reading it in wintry New England with your feet on the hearth; in a Florida fishing boat waiting for a snook; jammed in a New York subway; or on an Arizona mountain.

Opened traps, but Pinto patrols them. I am really angry about that cat and I am going to catch it somehow. Herman won't shoot it, although Rancher has weakly suggested this. Something has to be done! So I do it. Constructed a Cat Balchatri. A balchatri is a wire cage with nooses of fish line, used to catch hawks and owls, and sometimes shorebirds and herons, with adaptations. I used to take Sparrow hawks (oh, all right, you purists, kestrels) with them, but usually the mice I used for bait would get bored and chew the loops; so that when a hawk struck, or landed and walked around this interesting contraption he went scot-free. I brought two here with me, not thinking about how, if I should catch an owl at night, a prowling predator might get to it before I did; so I have not used them. They are not cat-sized, but they give me a model. I find a large wire box in the barn, use heavy test nylon, and make so many loops on its floor and sides that there is no way a cat can escape capture. Then I set out a similar, loopless decoy on the banding porch where Pinto is fed and bait it with sardines. We'll see about that cat!

January 7th

SUN! Heavy frost. Temperature 36 degrees. Did a large wash in the bathtub. Set out traps at 7:30; no takers. Cut back the trailing plants in my sunporch banding office. Rancher's Wife cherishes them but is too rarely here. Threw out the plastic ferns and a clay skull, then planted lettuce. Herman is here again, on my roof with more rolls of welcome protection. The peacocks are up with him, criticizing, and enjoying the sun.

There must be an easier route to Sycamore Canyon than how Herman has taken me, scrabbling over Rattlesnake Hill, inching down a steep cow trail. I could never lug net poles that way, nor get quickly back and forth as I'd need to. I don a sweater and the red quilted down vest that is this year's fashion (silly fashion—no sleeves). Off I go down Creek to where I have seen a cow path leading between two hills. As usual the way isn't as easy as it looked from a distance. I skirt cactus and do a lot of scrambling (one degree easier than scrabbling). Shortly I am sweating, and abandon the red vest. From where I am standing I can see the Ranch buildings, and Herman working about, but once over a hill it and the cow path are gone. To mark my way I tie ribbons on branches: I am on a featureless mesquite flat and will need guidance to return. I crash through brush, slide down a bank and am at Sycamore Creek, running shallowly, disappearing at times, meandering in the shelter of trees. I meander, too, the sun warm on my back. The hill I crossed shuts off Work and Responsibility. For an hour, for as long as I choose, I am on vacation. I wonder idly why warmth is equated with vacation? Few people I know head for cold country when they have time off, certainly not in winter. They want beaches, Florida, islands, Arizona (they read the same travel folders I did). And they bitch mightily, like me, if the weather deceives them.

I justify this morning excursion as a search for net lane possibilities or grassy open spaces that might provide me with sparrows. I come from a family of workaholics—we must always be Doing Something. Privately I classify my type of ornithology (pseudo-ornithology) with fishing. I am out of doors, in a spot of my own choosing, free to pick up and move. With luck I may hook a fish to take home for lunch. Or see a different bird. At this moment I am looking at an Acorn woodpecker, new for my list. This is to me definitely a step up from golf, although it lacks the physical exhilaration of tennis. It is surely less boring than jogging, although my pace contributes little to fitness. Hohum, I would rather look than think, so I amble along, just looking. Flocks of juncos mark my passage. Sunlight glints off boles and branches, whitens stones. Birds call and a breeze rustles leaves over my head. I encounter the cows, fenced off from me, and the grove of sycamores for which the Creek is named, with an old hawk's nest—the one Herman is sure is an eagle's. I hate to disappoint him.

No one knows where I am. I feel no sense of guilt, no driving need to follow the Creek to its source, high above. Besides, there is a fence across my way, tightly strung. So I go downhill, curious to see what lies around the next bend, and the ones after that. Sycamore Creek becomes entirely dry, joining Thomas Creek, still plashing sweetly over stones. Here is another sycamore tree, alone. A bank that might return me to the road to the Ranch is undercut and too steep to climb. So I retrace my steps, follow my ribbons, retrieve my red jacket, and am back in time for lunch.

Herman greets me sternly. All morning he has been eyeing that red vest motionless on its steep hillside. He had no binoculars to tell him if it enclosed me, collapsed or injured. I apologize meekly for my thoughtlessness, but inside my ego glows that he did not hotfoot it up in more than worry. I have passed some kind of test, or he would have come to make sure. Of course, he may just have been more concerned about our water lines. . . . I stir up a package of corn bread and take him half for his lunch.

January 11th

Rancher and Wife up overnight. Rancher is delighted with my balchatri trap. He has me make more and bigger loops to hang from its ceiling, as neck lassoos. Peggy is openly scornful. We set the contraption on the sunporch where I have been baiting Pinto, place a can of sardines in it, and peer through a window. Pinto quickly arrives, sniffing the delicious odor, walks into the trap and thoroughly enjoys his dinner. The loops snare nothing.

Peggy snorts again, runs out and through the garden, up the steps to the porch and manages, because Pinto trusts her, to slam the screen door before he can streak out. Doug edges in and with effort completes the catch with the fishing net I carry in my gear. Very useful for catching a bird loose in an aviary, never used for cats before. A solid month of frustration ended! Doug wires the cage shut and sets Pinto in the barn, where we can't hear his outraged yowling. There are eight hounds down at Doug's ranch, but I'll bet Pinto will be a match for them. I'm willing to bet he will show up here again someday, too.

January 15th. Letter to Amanda

"Left the screen door open for a moment to go for the ash bucket I share with Herman and return to a roomful of peacocks, inspecting to see if I make hospital corners on the bed, what is in the wastebasket, bathtub, mail carton, and What's Laid Out for Supper?

"Leave the door to the Banding Sunporch ajar and there they all are, scrutinizing a box of sparrow specimens Scott Mills supplied for my education, digging up my lettuce. . . . Catch a bird in a trap (at last Pinto the feral cat is gone, and hasn't yet found his way back) and they stand about it in a grave circle, wanting to know What Is This? And snatching the seeds a junco spatters out.

"My birds are mostly juncos, dammit. Two Canyon wrens. Bill owes me a sundowner apiece, he bet me I couldn't catch even one. I have a Bridled titmouse—an elegant bird like the titmouse in your Washington garden, only with a stylish black and white face; a Hermit thrush or two. No hummingbirds. I thought the Ranch would buzz with them.

"No mail in twelve days. I'd only have to answer it. So I have no idea what is going on in the Big World. News magazines arrive three weeks old. Yes, I have a radio, but it rarely gives national news, to my aggravation. I listen to it hopefully each morning while I eat my egg and outside the window a Gila woodpecker and a Bewick's wren share the peanut butter I smear on a tree for them. Sometimes when I am discouraged I sit with a book propped in front of me, gathering strength for what the day may bring, or probably won't bring. No need to hurry. Birds here don't fly until the sun comes over the hills to warm the trees and insects.

"The radio gives Tucson weather, which does not apply to this mountain range. Our weather comes from California, Tucson could use my services. Old Babo rises between me and the west. Today its top is wrapped in gray wool and I may shortly have to go out and close all those nets I opened before breakfast. This keeps my legs in trim, if not my disposition. Your Aunt Winifred refuses to believe it rains in Arizona and talks of visiting. I have news for her. No lying out in a deck chair in the sun under cloudless skies. Not here. Not this winter. Her beloved La Osa Ranch is down in the valley, only a mile from the border. Maybe their weather comes from Mexico."

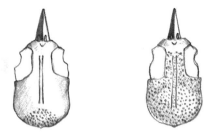

January 15th

Gray, dreary, but not cold—50 degrees (my values have changed). I opened the nets very early to see if this might improve my score. No, only two kinglets. The junco net has outlived its usefulness, they have learned to avoid it. I move it to the hill by the water tank.

I need to get juncos. When I examine the crowns of my avian victims to determine age I find only an occasional tick on a junco, and none at all on towhees. I would expect to, on ground-feeding birds. But I am seeing minuscule orange-red eggs (or parasites? I need a stronger glass) in or about the ears of juncos. I'll have to ask Scott about this, and keep track of how long the condition lasts, what the eggs hatch into. (Note: No one at the university could instruct me. Avian parasitology is pretty specialized. The condition continued a few weeks; after that, individuals recaptured did not show it.)

The age of a bird can often, but not always, be determined by the degree of ossification of its skull. Proper ornithologists term this "pneumatization"—an ugly word on the tongue, however correct. A bird has a double skull. As a chick matures, the thin columns of bone ossifying between the two layers can be seen with a strong magnifying glass. They look like dots of salt. They increase as the bird ages, at differing rates and in differing patterns for different species. Some birds' skins are too thick or too dark to see through, some species never wholly pneumatize. Some, like kinglets, do early; some late. The Banding Laboratory requires information as to whether a bird is in its Hatching Year or Adult (the general term for after Hatching Year, which ends, arbitrarily, January 1). Also, if we can determine this, we record Second, Third, of After Third Year as indicated by plumage changes, eye color, degree of molt, feather wear. Not too much is known definitively about these, but as more study is done and birds of known year of banding are recovered, we are learning. Slowly. All science is slow.

Skulling a bird takes delicate handling and patience. I wet the crown feathers to expose the skin. Afterward, on cold days, I breathe warmly on these feathers to dry them before I release the birds. So they won't get pneumonia. Obviously they don't, there are banded juncos all over the place, usually right back in the net. It is on separating the crown feathers that I find ticks and parasites.

Jays have thick skins, dark, but I feel I can age them. The fully Adult have black bills, and their backs are concolor blue. Immatures have the bill yellow in varying degrees, and the wing coverts are faded and brown, retained from juvenile plumage. But the Banding Laboratory writes me there is not yet enough information to know when the changes to full maturity take place, so I must not report these ostensibly young ones as Hatching Year.

I will have to return next winter and catch the same ones again. Or rather, definitely to learn, I will have to handle birds recently flown from the nest for one, two, probably three years.

Time, that's what research takes. Time and infinite patience. Bill Robertson, my beloved mentor in south Florida, has been studying Bald eagles and Sooty tern for twenty years, and is still reluctant to publish a definitive paper on their life patterns. I am just a one-shot playgirl. (Though I'll bet a nickel I am right on those jays.)

Wing coverts and tails are important factors in aging birds. You must look at them for color, contrast, fading, degree of wear, shape, edgings. When my Painted buntings in Florida lost a tail feather or two through mischance, the replacements grew in in the original juvenile color. This confused me plenty until, from handling over a thousand, I learned.

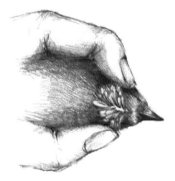

January 17th

If this account deals chiefly and interminably with weather it is because when you live in the country weather is what controls your life. In cities you are insulated by cement and elevators and subways and taxis and revolving doors, with heat that rises at the flick of a finger, with vast machines that clear the streets of snow and broken branches. I will conveniently forget my thirty winters in Buffalo, where, if our Wage Earner was to get to work, lanes had to be shoveled through drifts to the garage, and during the day I had to clear the walls of slush and ice those same vast machines plugged his evening ingress with. I remember, too, skids and traffic snarls, and lying on my back in a new coat in a slushy gutter to reaffix a tire chain, and some winters hauling groceries home on a sled. But like power shortages these are results of our artificial civilization, to be greeted with a snarl, or as an adventurous break in routine; to be photographed and written about in newspapers. In the country weather is daily, controlling you, not you it. And no one writes it up. But me.

I wake in the night to rain pounding on the roof, slapping the windows. What, again? I had written reports late, until the propane lamp cylinder gave out. I think now of this work, and of my plan to drive to Tucson to pick up two weeks' mail. I should be thinking of bird nets out in the rain, but lulled by the storm I turn over and go back to sleep.

At 7:00 A.M. I need a flashlight to read the clock. A wind lifts the metal sheetings off the big oil drum trash cans and whams them across the yard. I had placed heavy rocks on these, for such mischance. I remember now that when I arrived each sheeting had *two* rocks, placed by Herman. Too late . . . Now my mind jumps to those nets in that wash fed by the Rhyolite Cliffs high above. I pull on clothes, build a fire, roll up Gene's rug against a muddy return, and am off. Water is running, waterfalls stream in every declivity. The peacocks, or the wind, have knocked over the benches on the Big House porch. The birds are sullenly lined up on them, still under the roof, but wet. Even Banty does not sound his cheery call, nor thank me as I toss out grain. Maybe in my leaky slicker and hood they don't recognize me as their Happy Companion and Source of Supply. What about the other day, my friends, when I left the cabin door open and returned to find all ten of you crowded into my small room?

Back in the cabin again I turn on the radio, set to Tucson, and get San Diego. That's what atmospheric disturbance does for you. Well, no one is going to arrive with a picnic lunch and mail today, so what does it matter what Tucson has to say about weather? I place another stick of mesquite on the crackling fire.

While I write this I am conducting an experiment. Man puts chemicals into his atmosphere with unpredictable results, as we are discovering. What, equally, does he do to his food? Off and on during my thirty-five days here I have been eating tasty slices from a—one—loaf of bread. Let me hasten to explain that I make my own bread as routinely as I make my bed and scrub the sink. I have had to, every since our boys returned from a Canadian summer and challenged me with tales of a teen-age girl who kneaded bread dough for the camp table. If she could turn out this delicious staple for fifty camp lads every day, all summer, kneeling in front of a wooden tub, plunging her arms in and out, why couldn't Mother? Why must our family pay fifteen whole cents (this was forty years ago) to the bakerman who rattled down our street in his wagon afternoons, demanding exact change for a product fit only for spitballs? I was suspicious that the boys' real motivation was their reluctance continually to have to loan me that "exact change," nickels and dimes that I never seemed to have, but they out-talked me. I gave baking bread a try. And never again was I permitted to serve commercial stuff, no matter how mine turned out (you can always call it "peasant bread").

The fragrance of bread baking perfumes a home for hours, lingering. Kneading—pushing and twisting the dough as you would potter's clay—is a pleasure to the hands. Proper bread is nutritious. At least mine is, concocted of bran, rolled oats, whole wheat, soy or other flours according to my whim, eggs, onion, cheese, seeds, herbs. A small loaf hot from the oven is gone by the end of tea-time.

Store bread, however excellent this loaf of Pepperidge Farm, Whole Wheat, Thin Sliced may be, came up with my supplies only to use until my kitchen was organized. It has lasted because I have eaten it only as a Special Treat, or have misplaced the knife I use for my homemade bread. Sometimes it has lived in its pliofilm wrapper in the fridge; sometimes, as in the last three days, it has been out on the counter to be fed to the birds, which I didn't. You would think that by now the slices left would be dry and moldy. Not at all.

This becomes a double experiment. My boxlike toaster, built like a slanting hat crown, is unsatisfactory. So I put a slice of this remarkably long-lived bread on the perforated metal lids I recently bought to give my stove burners a third speed. (The other two are On and Off, there was no Simmer.) To see if this lid might serve as a toaster and if, incredibly, the magic ingredients man has invented for food preservation still worked. Yes. Five weeks after purchase, delicious. Slightly burned, but then all my food is.

It is now 9:30 A.M. and if I am to see where the lines are on this paper I must light the lamp. A Hermit thrush is investigating the grain I have thrown out. To see what the Miller puts in *his* sustenance to keep it fresh?

January 18th. Unless it is the 19th, my days run together. Amanda's Birthday. Letter to the Spoffords

"I must say your State has abominable weather. And I haven't done anything for The Conservancy worth the gas used to bring me here. I can plod down the road to my VW—I had to wade twice over my booted ankles today—and not see a damned bird. When I haul myself up and down the slopes to the next canyon the same flocks of juncos and finches that are here are over there, I see their shiny bands. All I have done for science is to confirm the winter population, which Bill and Scott knew before I came. Had my first hummer today, though—probably an Anna's, feeding at a verbena that made the mistake of blooming.

"I get exercise bringing in firewood, and moving nets from here to there, the birds learn their locations quickly. I amuse myself roasting potatoes in the ashes—the way I used to with Frederic Law Olmsted's nieces, three little girls making bonfires in the autumn under an enormous copper beech; long ago, in Brookline, Massachusetts. Can't wait for migration. When does it start?

"I'll come to town for the Raptor Meeting unless there is more rain. If it's under water there is a broad wash I'm scared to cross. Joe Hickey will be there with his new wife, I want to meet her. Can we all have supper in some Mexican joint?

"Two quail hunters took my mail out yesterday. What were they doing up here? Inside our posted gate? They drove me down to my VW to make sure it was still there. Intact, a welcome sight. Otherwise I have seen no one. Bill is East, and no one in his right mind would come up here this week. Hope you have survived. All I do is eat and sleep. It's awful."

January 20th. Letter to Anne and Vic Rose

"Yesterday I had to close my nets because it was *hailing*. This is the desert? Lower Sonoran? And this morning was 32 degrees. I played with my toys.

"The trees on Baboquivari are snow-covered. There is a skim of ice on the old pots and pans Rancher's Wife scatters everywhere for the peacocks to drink from. I can't net birds in this weather. They need every bit of their energy to stay alive, not to be pestered for scientific purposes. Even on a normal day if it is chilly a feathered scrap like a kinglet or a verdin will collapse in my hand, or cling to my warm fingers when I release it. I have a remedy for this. I tuck the bird down my front, where it just fits in that cosy, sweatered hollow. Warmed and revived it will scritch and scratch, demanding to get out. I hadn't figured on Cold when I volunteered to do this study. I was thinking in terms of subtropical Florida.

This afternoon the sky had cleared but the wind was strong, the Creek running swift and deep. I hoped my postman-grocery-delivery boy might appear from Tucson, but by lunch time he hadn't, so I put on my boots and headed for the tallest hill between me and the Rhyolite Ridge, to see what lies beyond. More canyons, more ridges, I know. Of course. A Cooper's hawk, hunting. Three layers of woollens make for clumsiness.

"There are two basic rules here in climbing: 1) When you slither, do not grab the nearest bush to save yourself—all bushes in Arizona have thorns; 2) If you stop to observe a bird—my job—set yourself firmly against said slithering. The bird will turn out to be a sparrow, and by the time your binoculars are focused it won't be there. Or your hands will be shaking so from crawling over shaly rocks that you can't focus.

"I am learning the advantages of following cattle trails. With their many meandering switchbacks they never look as if they would lead me to my goals, but I have never arrived by a route of my own, scratched and puffing and knee-sore, where there has not been ample sign of bovine life before me. Today's hill, once I achieved its summit, had a group of shade-giving mesquite (in summer, not now), an understory of cow dung, and a sweeping view all the way to Mexico—ridge on ridge descending to Altar Valley and then far down the desert. The Rhyolites at my back blocked any view in that direction, but I see a saddle in them that I mean to get through next time. It is not too much further as the raven flies, or that pair of Golden eagles riding the updrafts back and forth across the pitted faces of the cliffs.

"A young person would make these laborious climbs speedily, but I don't trust my gimpy hip, and must constantly be aware that if I fall there is no one to pick me out of the cactus, or even to miss me. Obviously cattle had gone up this hill, making paths. Going down, though, it appeared to have been each cow for itself, with only a few indications of community effort and, I assume, a final slide on the rear end. At least that is how I finished, finding myself in an arroyo full of waterfalls. That is when, looking straight up in the blue air above me, I saw the eagles. Worth every thorn and cactus spine."

January 24th

I have been alone now for two weeks. Gray, grisly. Made bread. Started on my IRS figures. Done my usual chores.

"Good spirits will not dwell where there is dust," preached Mother Ann, founder of the Shakers in 1774. I am in need of good spirits. Rain, rain.

Thought for the day:

> Communication is the exchange of information between two or more minds. (Definition.) If one takes an objective and careful look at man's communication with man, woman's communication with woman, and man's communication with woman, we see that most intraspecies interpersonal communication is not ideal. (*J. C. Lilly, The Mind of the Dolphin*)

My reading is a pleasure to me. Dr. Lilly observed more than dolphins in his Miami Laboratory.

At dusk I look out into the gathering night, seated as always on that hard chair, elbows on the metal table. The window reflects the orange in the rock walls, the orange quilt and china, the pictures that make this cabin a home. More than my sherry warms me. I am dreaming.

"Don't look back," well-meaning friends used to advise me, and sometimes still do when I regale them with tales of riding a camel with Brad on Karachi beaches, of being taken into custody in Kashmir for birdwatching at the airport, of faux pas I regularly made at diplomatic dinners. Of that Peruvian twilight when, rain-soaked and desperate, I lingered at the edge of a great declivity at Machu Picchu, wondering how many over the years before me might have taken the jump that tempted me; weighing my widowed grief, the advantages of instant peace against a dutiful need to rejoin my comrades at the hotel. A young soldier with a Georgia accent brought me back. How did he know?

"Ma'am?" he said, appearing at my side. "Ma'am?" Touching my arm very lightly he turned me back into living. Alas, there is always someone to bring you back.

"Forget the past," admonish the heavy-handed. "That part of your life is gone, a closed book. Put it on the shelf. Here, have a drink. Do you play bridge?"

I learned not to wince at their kindly intent, to meet their eyes. But how could I—can I—put to gather dust on a shelf all those years of my life radiant with children's voices, their father stamping snow from his boots on winter evenings, returning to the warmth and love of his home? I am to shut away thirty years of happiness? The books by my fireplace at home are mostly from the parts of my life that are gone—*Peter Rabbit* and Arthur Rackham, *The Wind in the Willows;* Vincent Millay and Brooks Atkinson; Sylvia Ashton-Warner, Robert Frost, Brad's friend Andy (E. B.) White, who used a few of my anecdotes back in the days of the 1930 Depression, when *The New Yorker* was an upstart. Sherry in hand, fire crackling,

I often take them down to be comforted by the echoes of long ago years.

Two weeks alone, cold on a mountain, is a long time. Looking out into the dark tonight I open this book I have never closed, riffle its pages. Pausing, skipping, looking back, far away from Arizona. I do not lack for company.

A mouse scampers. Wind rattles the vines outside. I do not lack for data that need putting into order, either, I remind myself. I set aside the sherry glass and reach for a pencil.

January 25th

An inch and a half of rain during the night. Probably more, the peacocks have tilted the gauge. Those darned birds can't let anything alone! Even the nearest hills are swathed in clouds. The mean rainfall at the University of Arizona in Tucson over sixty-nine years was 11.4 inches, with about 35 percent of this falling from December to March (Herbert Brandt's *Arizona and its Birdlife,* 1964). The rains, of course, fall irregularly from year to year. Some characterize them as "gentle, soaking rains." Ho! I have not kept careful track but so far my records read 10.9 inches plus two days not recorded, plus one day of "rain spits" plus one day with "hail and rain." That's in five weeks. I didn't have a gauge the first week I was here. (I could have used it indoors as well as out.) How am I ever going to cross those Creeks on Saturday? I wash my hair and bundle my mail defiantly. I *am* going! I should have read Mr. Brandt's big book before I rushed west. He also informs me that the average winter minimum temperature in Tucson back then was about 22 degrees, and on one terrible day sixty-six years ago it dropped to −6 degrees.

I make a mug of tea and read further that the average sunshine in the period was 85 percent, or ten hours a day. Do you hear that, Baboquivari, up there in your clouds?

January 26th. Morning

Tomorrow I am going Outside. That is, I plan to go Outside, but it has rained on and off for two days, snow is low and heavy on the mountain. This means that if it warms—only I see ice on the peacock pans—those many high arroyos will feed the Creek. This is already running briskly, I can hear it through the walls. Water from the mountains pours down into and through all those many DIPS, DO NOT ENTER that cross my way to the city. I am often warned about them. "Carry a book and a sandwich; or two. And wait. Hours. Maybe a day."

Clouds are spreading now, up from the valley, blanking out the sunny blue I breakfasted by. Tucson forecasts "possible rain." Bill knows I *must* leave. I have a National Audubon board meeting in San Diego. He might just come to fetch me, but I know he is leading a field trip tomorrow and has meetings to attend. I heard talk about a hearing in Phoenix, too. Today? He is involved in so much, trying to save some of Arizona from blind development. He isn't against development, having moved out here from the East himself, he just thinks there should be planning, discrimination. So I am on my own, as I have proclaimed all along I wish to be. You say it, Lady, you pay for it . . .

My social clothes are in Tucson, but I am going to need warm ones also. I will be visiting climates from the Salton Sea to Stinson Beach north of San Francisco, which in February is not warm. A full briefcase stands at the door. I need a bag for overnights, dry foot gear to put on after the Creeks are waded. I must take packs and insulated bags to carry up food on my return. Far too much for one trip to the car, so I start collecting. It might be raining tomorrow on that two-mile run, I had better carry down all I can today.

Afternoon:

I waited too long. Snow! Not heavy, but enough to coat the horses waiting at the gate for an apple handout. They are so cold, and doubtless miserable, that one, Spooky, doesn't even hide behind bushes but stands and gazes at me mournfully. I have no apples.

I waste time at the Creek trying to improve my path of stepping stones. The current rolls these additions away. I roll up my heavy wool pants (Eddie Bauer finally produced some. They are tough as iron and warm; I live in them) and splash across. Halfway to the second ford the sun comes out. I shed my waterproofing and mentally revamp my travel wardrobe, forgetting that this is irrevocably in the sacks I am putting in the car. As I return, stumping up the Canyon in clumsy but waterproof boots, the snow starts again. It is pretty on the oak trees on the mountain, like a heavy hoar frost.

February 17th. Letter to my brother, Stephen, and wife, Marion

"I am back in my wintry brown and purple ridges after a blissful month in California. I must admit to enjoying fine china, silver, evening fires that aren't hidden inside a stove, candlelight that is decoration only; oysters and good wine and good talk and bowls of ice cream; newspapers and catching up on the political U.S. All entirely normal to you, but mighty different from life on my mountain. As Jane Austen wrote in a book buried in my college years: 'I do not mind having what is too good for me.'

"After I last wrote you January was cold, and dull living. The morning I took off my water pipes were frozen solid, it was snowing hard. I met Rancher Brother driving in to see if I was frozen solid, too, and dumped the problems on him. Tucson was blanketed in snow. Children rolled and shouted, sucked the astonishing white stuff, carried it indoors to their mothers. Refugees from Minnesota and Michigan were disgruntled, to put it mildly.

"In sybaritic elegance I lunched at the Arizona Inn with my Vassar roommate of fifty years ago. Flowers! Tablecloths and napkins! Well-dressed, attentive young waiters! WARM! Stuffed and happy I set out for San Diego, clad in wool from toe to top, my car heater going full blast. Might as well have been driving out your New England lane, instead of along the border of Mexico.

"For two days in San Francisco I was threatened with a hospital. With my car parked illegally in the Sheraton lot in San Diego, hiding (I hoped) under its coat of mud? With my checkbook on Baboquivari, with our Big Sister about to leave on a cruise? She never blinked, bless her, and when I could eat again made up for my scare with scallops and mushrooms and chocolates and more ice cream, disapproving the canned diet I must return to. I stopped at the Salton Sea Refuge as you had suggested. It was a warm, blue day, peaceful after the cities. Thousands of snow geese rested in glistening white flocks on glistening, rain-soaked green grass. On the island a Burrowing owl popped out of a hole in the rocks, gave me a long stare, and popped back in again.

"The hills of suburban southern California were golden— miles of acacia trees in full bloom where I visited Vic and Anne Rose. I never believe my pollen allergy until it has me limp and lifeless. I managed the drive back to Tucson on a diet of rum-and-honey-lemonade, and have been lying about, thumbing listlessly through mail and magazines, at the Roes. The cat keeps my chest warm, Bill makes distressed sounds, baffled by my lack of spirit, Alice as usual sees to my comfort and requests for paperclips and stamps. Henry reads me his books, and crayons pictures for my wall. Where was that friendly doctor when I needed him? He sent me off with a parting admonition of being sure to eat enough, elderly people often don't. (Elderly indeed! He should see me packing supplies in!) Since my remedy for loneliness, for depression, for tired legs, for early-up-at-dawn is eating, I had laughed at him, and promised. He should have known from my shape that this is not a hazard.

It was a very satisfactory trip, just the cure for a woman with cabin fever. Maybe the weather will be improved by the time I am back up mountain. Maybe even the road will be improved. Maybe it won't, the propane truck can't get to the ranch and I will have to snowshoe back to Cape Cod.

February 18th. Letter to Sally Spofford

"Don't ever expect, my girl, that you can go away and come back, even to a remote mountain, without something having happened. What had happened here was that in my absence the wind again blew out the pilot on the fridge, and all the meat, chicken, cheese, etc. that I have no replacements for had to be shoveled out. You wouldn't believe the stench, even before I opened the cabin door. Everything had to be scrubbed, and aired for hours. Bill took the mess far off and buried it. *Siempre hay una mosca en la sopa,* but this was a larger *mosca* than necessary!

"Still voiceless and coughing, but on the mend. Beautiful day, no rain. The men assure me spring is just around the corner. What I want are leaves on the mesquite to shade nets, so I will catch some of those migrants everyone advertises.

"Bill brought friends up with me to picnic, Alice stayed home with the children. We missed her; Alice adds grace to any group. The men went off exploring. Avoiding the odoriferous cabin Mary and I sat in the sun on the Big House porch. We saw an Anna's hummingbird darting about hunting flowers so I boiled some red syrup, hung a feeder on a rafter, and within minutes the three-gram, scarlet-headed mite thrummed to it, stoking."

(Note: It was March before I saw another. Anna's are vertical migrants, wintering in warm valleys where flowers are available, breeding in higher altitudes. Mostly they winter in California although a few are reported in southwest Arizona. It must be a hostile environment for them, and certainly at this date Thomas Canyon is! The species was named for the Duchess of Rivoli, whom Audubon described as "a beautiful young woman, not more than twenty, extremely graceful and polite." Elegant wife of a marshal of France under Napoleon, I wonder what she would think of me in my worn slacks? The Duke's name is on another hummer, the Rivoli. He would think the same.)

February 20th

The third warm, sunny day. I would have stayed longer in California but Bill and Scott had told me birds should be migrating by the end of February. My New England conscience made me return to have everything in good order for a deluge of feathered visitors (and human, if the road should have been repaired). Marvelous prospects, both. I am cured enough so I can do some honest labor and start again to earn my keep. (Note: Spring arrived in April.)

Forty degrees outside at 7:00, warmer in, no need to build a fire. I put water on for coffee and go out to open, untangle, adjust the nearest nets. At any normal banding station you catch birds from earliest light to midmorning, but not here. Except for the junco net—in the open by the Big House where the peacocks feed, wood is chopped, and the old yellow truck sits on flat tires—catching a bird here is a happenstance that occurs at any hour. Fortified by two eggs and jam I go to work. I am here for ornithological purposes, not to wash dishes, sweep, make a bed, do laundry, separate cans from bottles from trash in the barrels where an Episcopal Youth Retreat blithely dumped them in my absence.

By midmorning I am discouraged. The nets are in fine order, but empty. Before I went away I took down the junco net, located where Rancher likes to park his truck. I think I am seeing fewer juncos now. If I set it up again I can find out if this is fact or imagination.

Setting up a net in this rocky soil with only one pair of hands, knees, and set of teeth is not as easy as the finished product appears to the visitors who think I lead a cushy life. The task involves pick, shovel, sledgehammer, rake, a ball of nylon twine, adrenalin, and cuss words. Unsecured, a pole tips, the net slackens into a patch of nightshade with pretty yellow berries and branched stems. These berries are so evil that even the peacocks don't eat them. Each one must be picked out as patiently as a bird. Midway through the struggle the horses arrive to help. I am to them the Apple Lady, so they are delighted to join me. They don't belong in the yard; the bars were left down yesterday by mistake.

Two students coming down from four days on the Peak had signed out, chatted a bit, and then hurried on, to return in disarray. They had found their truck broken into, money, packs, camera lenses gone. Far more serious, their light switch had been flipped, their battery was dead. I could offer gasoline money and sympathy, but not mechanical assistance. By extraordinary luck Rancher Brother was here, riding on the hills, to celebrate the federal date of Washington's Birthday. He drove us down to the windmill, and after several abortive attempts owing to lack of tools, everyone's hurry, and the lads' excitement, they managed to go bottom-scraping off. In his haste Rancher Brother forgot his binoculars, and to set up the horse bars. So here at my shoulder are my two equine friends, bigger than I, wanting to get through the net into any hay leavings in their corral.

Those bars are a nuisance. Every half hour I must crawl through them. So, when I have persuaded my big pals outside, I decide to replace only one. And find immediately why Rancher uses two. Animals are as smart as people—some people, anyway. Birds too, I reflect dismally, having caught none all day.

I comfort myself by potting the parsley and pansies and petunias brought up in Bill's Wagoneer. They will live safely inside my Banding Office where the peacocks can't nibble on them (if I keep the door hooked). When the nights warm up I will hang the petunias outside for hummingbirds' breakfasts. A scattering of verbena is now in bloom along the arroyos— marvelously fragrant, mornings. Bill's sharp eyes saw a few anemones in bloom coming up the road, harbingers of spring. The Spoffords get woodpeckers, orioles, tanagers, grosbeaks, finches—more than a score of species coming to their sugar water (they don't bother with petunias) as well as a buzzing swarm of hummers. In Tucson house finches drink Alice's offerings dry. I ought to get Something.

I caught a road runner! Sauntering up Sparrow Hill after lunch, no rush (I'd had no birds all day), I saw a sparrow struggling in a net. Caught birds usually lie quiet. Then I saw there were two sparrows, agitated, and no wonder! Between them was a great, ungainly creature that up to now I have glimpsed only once or twice, skittering across the road. I didn't know how to handle it. Road runners have long, powerful bills for eating snakes and lizards; big feet, long talons. A heron with its long bill will strike for your eyes, is dangerous. The sharp talons of hawks must be controlled with great care, they can cripple a hand. Gingerly disentangling this problem I found it a flaccid critter that rolled its eyes as if to say: "Who, me? Going for those sparrows for lunch? Not at all, I was just passing by."

I could photograph only its head. I work my camera with one hand (and my chin, or knee), holding a bird in the other. My arm isn't long enough to focus even on a flicker, much less a road runner. Fortunately my interest is in the shapes and colors of birds' heads, wings, bills, eyes. You take what you can get in this world. If it is a road runner you are lucky! Their feet have two talons pointing forward, two back—the Indians say so you can't tell from their tracks which way they are going.

At dusk I watch a Bewick's wren dust-bathing outside my

window. Fashioning a small hollow where leaves have softened the ground somewhat, the bird flicked particles of dust and dirt about with its wings the way a robin does water. It paused, resumed with energy, paused again, flicked, fluffed its feathers a moment, and flew off into the shadows.

Two days ago I saw a Canyon wren do the same. A pair of these wrens have an opening into the Big House. As light fails I often see them skitter along the porch rafters, then pop into some interior roost, safe from the night and the weather. But this one flew suddenly down onto a clear space packed hard by vehicles, in front of the steps. It worked stubbornly at nestling into the ground, agitated its wings as if bathing. Then it moved to a better hollow, more successfully.

No one seems sure of the function of dust-bathing. It must rid the feathers somewhat of external parasites; perhaps it increases feather insulation. It is seen more among birds of open country that are not water bathers—bobwhites, pheasants, larks, even some hawks and owls. It is fairly common among wrens, even more so among house sparrows. These latter really kick up a dust storm, and may bathe as a communal activity. I read somewhere (Forbush? It was in New England) of a farmer who set out wood ashes in a tray for whip-poor-wills to dust in. I'll have to try it; I have plenty of ashes. Just no whip-poor-wills, and the winds would soon scatter my offering. I have never seen peacocks bathe in anything.

February 21st

A small owl in a net has me enormously excited. Owls are always exciting, and difficult to get out, sharp claws making hamburger of my hands, bills snapping. The big book on *Ari-*

zona Birds I run to shows three pages of small owls, with several names for most of them. I am confused. Besides, I haven't yet had breakfast.

I should have taken more time, had that cup of coffee, read more carefully. Then I might not have missed the line that informs on the salient difference between the similar Screech and Whiskered owls. This is the pattern of the inside edge of the outside primary (wing feather). I told you differences in bird species are subtle. The Whiskered owl is the rare one up here, not yet documented, so of course I decide that is what I am holding in my hand as I leaf through my books. I photograph it thoroughly (although not, alas, that outer feather) and let it go back to its hole in the oak tree.

"What am I to do if I get an unusual bird?" I had asked the men. "Drive to town to fetch you? Bring it to Tucson in a paper bag, then back here to release it?"

I don't have time to train homing pigeons, which was their suggestion.

(Note: My identification was disallowed, to everyone's regret. Later I caught a second owl in the same spot. By then I had been instructed in that barred—or unbarred—feather edge. This second bird was definitely a Screech; probably they were a resident pair. Their markings in Arizona are slightly different from those that lived in a hole in my Florida avocado tree.)

February 22nd, George's Birthday

The net up Canyon beyond the verdin nest took jays, a woodpecker, and at noon a cow. I have now seen two hummingbirds, and two days ago I netted a female *Selasphorus* (a kind of

hummingbird). There are two *Selasphorus* (accent on the *as*)—
the Allen's and the Rufous. The females are almost identical,
and those of two other species are also very similar. Knowing
my catch to be out of normal range at this season, and that I
would suffer a barrage of questions, I photographed it every
way to Sunday—head, bill, wings, tail spots, belly; in this
light and that. It died in my hand. I was upset.

(Note: The Museum men were overjoyed. The bird turned
out to be a state record, whatever its identity, and photographs
would not have been sufficient. Two months later, when I left
Arizona, Gale Monson and Alan Phillips, who wrote *Arizona
Birds* (Joe Marshall was the third author) still hadn't agreed
on the classification. The specimen was sent to the Curator of
Birds at the San Diego Museum, Amadeo Rea, for his opinion,
and was argued over again and again. Finally, Gale wrote me
in June, they decided it was a *Sasin* (Allen's) but reluctantly.

Afternoon:

Banty is gone. For three days now that fine, first-light crow
has been missing. It would start far off up Canyon, barely
audible; approach; then sound with a final cheery ring at my
door. He rarely woke me, I would be deep under blankets
watching light grow in the east window. When I dashed outside to read the thermometer he would be waiting for his
handout. The peacocks tolerated him but kept him on their
outskirts, rattling their tails at him. Early he learned I was an
admiring friend, always with a handful of grain, but I could
not tame him to my hand. Hikers photographed him three
days ago. They had never before seen the glory of a Bantam
rooster and were enchanted. I look for his bright feathers under
oak trees up and down the wash but find nothing. A bobcat?
Fox? Horned owl? Age? He must have been old, Frances

brought him here. My mornings are drearier, and it is dreary enough here, gray and cold. I fight off depression with work. On sunny days I am full of zip and happiness.

(Note: That night and for many nights thereafter the peacocks deserted their usual night roosts, were flighty and nervous at dusk, moved back and forth across the Creek, even some nights roosting up the wash by Sparrow Hill. It was more than two weeks before they returned to their usual tree, hollering and hoohawing at each other until sometimes *I* would holler at *them*. Surprised, they would fall silent. For a time.)

February 24th

A gale is blowing from the north, the sun comes and goes behind cumulus clouds, the thermometer has inched up only to 50 degrees. Understandably, none of those visitors who talked of coming to camp over the holiday weekend have showed.

I have run eleven nets for two days, taking nothing but an indignant jay and three or four repeating Oregon juncos that stayed behind when the large flock of their brethren went north. Smart of them; the weather may be more clement up there. The peacocks are huddled under a bush, waiting for spring. Jays are clinging madly to twigs too thin for their weight, trying to get at seed in those small pottery feeders I use in the hope jays *can't* get at them. I don't mind bringing seed up mountain for them (as long as it comes with Bill, not on my back), but their appetites are tremendous. Let them eat caterpillars. Besides, they are choosy and take only sunflower kernels, spilling the cheaper grain out for the peacocks and a scruffy ground squirrel that has emerged from hibernation to share the wealth.

Ground squirrel! Suddenly alert, I study this addition to my yard. Like the anemones Bill saw he is a true harbinger of the spring I impatiently await. Unlike bears and chipmunks and other creatures that sleep their winters away, rousing from time to time to defecate or to nibble on their winter stores, to shift position, probably grumbling like me at the length of winter, ground squirrels are genuine hibernators. Like bats, woodchucks, some jumping mice, and the poor-wills I am hoping to net. Programmed to save energy, one cold fall day in its burrow this squirrel would have become torpid, its respiration slowing from 100 to 4, body temperature dropping dramatically from 97 degrees (like us when we are cold and tired) to 39 degrees, which we fortunately don't attain. His reserves must carry him until a certain time, even this cold day with its gales blowing triggers his reappearance above ground. No wonder after months of suspended animation this untidy fellow is vacuuming up my unexpected bounty! And if he is out, now skunks, that are only sleepers, soon should be too.

And the poor-wills. Exciting thought. I will leave the tops of some nets open at night, high enough so no predator can reach to them, and try my luck (for poor-wills, not skunks).

I toss a cup of seed to my new companion, return to the window, and watch him hunt. I compare his energy saving with that of small birds who must tide themselves through the cold and foodless hours of night. My eastern chickadees are programmed with similar physiological changes, and here hummingbirds and probably those kinglets that I revive inside my sweaters mornings. If I could find these small creatures in the dark I could pluck them, torpid and unresisting, from the branches of their roosts. How many other species? What a lot of things there are to study!

A bird's breathing is correlated to its wing strokes, each stroke using energy that must be replaced. A pigeon's breathing jumps from thirty times a minute at rest to four hundred and fifty in flight; a hummingbird's from two hundred and fifty at rest to an uncountable number, a hazy blur of motion. How can a hummingbird stoke enough nectar, enough infinitestimal insects up here where there are so few flowers, to power its zooming energy? I don't know how ornithologists have measured the above statements, I just read their articles, many of them doubtless out of date as more and more graduate students explore the field. As a young man that marvelous Dr. Alexander Wetmore counted 1,119 feathers on a Ruby-crowned kinglet one October. It would have to be a dedicated student to try to update that effort. Not me, even with time heavy on my hands. Besides, my birds are alive.

Long ago, before I knew enough to keep track of names and journal issues, I read that a scientist studying a Ruby-throated hummingbird's intake and output of energy in a glass bell had gravely calculated there was no way such a mite could store up enough to fly the Gulf of Mexico. Yet they do, by the thousands, twice a year. That for your scientists and their glass bells!

Afternoon:

I am content to be indoors today, stoking my small stove, stewing on it soup and a pan of pears that after a week on the window sill were still as hard as stones. Modern packaging irritates. I've had apples for a month, bought packaged, that still aren't edible. Maybe I will stew *them.* Anything to put off working up my IRS data. Or answering the mail.

I get a lot of mail. My friends live all around the country. I like them, I bum on them when I travel. It seems only fair to let them know where I am living so they needn't worry I will show up on their doorsteps. They are welcome to bum on me too, and fortunately some of them do, but a rule of life seems to be that you can rarely repay those who do you a kindness, you can only pass along their generosity. I am on several Conservation boards, which means a lot of correspondence. Audubon is the one that really inundates me, because its interests are so far-flung. You can't protect wildlife, which is where Audubon started, without preserving its habitats. Nowadays this involves you with oil spills and energy; polluted air and rivers; mining for shale oil and phosphate and coal and uranium; protection of wetlands and forests and beaches and Alaska and tropical forests, not to mention fertile land on which to grow our food; the effect on the air we breath of huge industrial complexes sometimes next door, sometimes many hundreds or thousands of miles away; the effect of the chemicals we broadcast so lavishly for agriculture (10,000 robins estimated dead in one potato field outside Homestead, Florida; millions of breeding birds killed in one year in New Brunswick, Canada from the use of pesticides that after many years have not yet controlled the spruce budworm). Ultimately this all comes down to the prime cause of man's problems—lack of population control. A big field to cover.

Board members are supposed to know everything. At least that's what chapter officers think. I get exposed to a lot of chapter officers as I travel around, and disappoint them. As I've said, I am a field, not a policy person; my interest is ornithological research. I have been reluctant to go on Boards, but who can resist the flattery, and the education they give? It certainly generates a lot of mail, and I feel I must answer it. Sometimes a personal letter does more than the formal communications organizations send out to explain their purposes and funding needs. You never know. You just have to hope, and keep on plugging for what you care about. I love the people I meet, and so far have survived, but my postage bill is horrific.

February 24th. Letter to granddaughter Molly

"Are you still there? If ever Bill, or someone, gets up I hope there are lots of letters from you and your Mama. Bill was to come over the holiday with family and friends but it rained. No one, not even Rancher, has showed since I returned a week ago.

"I came back with a bronchial attack from all those flowering trees in your California. If I am allergic to mesquite flowers they will have to carry me out of here in a box, mesquite is what these hills have on them. It is blowing like crazy, and cold. I build up the fire and am staying in, eating all day because I get so bored working on figures. You never got your mathematical genes from *me*. Am about to have a healthy supper of yogurt (ugh) and canned peaches that need eating, and the last of the prunes with some good health cereal Ian Nisbet left me two months ago. Don't be jealous.

"Can you read this? I am writing by the light of two big Christmas candles. Pretty but useless, the flames burn inside. A ten-cent votive candle is better. I had a lovely time with your father. We didn't talk about anything, just were together, walked on those headlands beyond Bolinas, napped on the edge of a cliff. I should have stayed on with him."

February 25th. Letter to Sally Spofford

"Huzza! My daily Gila woodpecker has finally discovered the peanut butter I smear on a tree outside this window. Only he has been hanging in the same position for twenty minutes. Maybe it gave him a tummy ache?

"I have been getting nothing, from 7:00 A.M. to 6:00 P.M., so today I am tending to desk work. It is blowing a gale. My mailbox spilleth over again. My head is swelled by requests for reprints of a Roof-nesting tern article I published years ago. They still come, from Kuala Lumpur, Portugal, Finland, Spain, and Scotland, as well as from around the U.S. Ah, Ego! How would we get through the day without it?

"When you come—WHEN—bring your sleeping bags and stay, instead of just a picnic sandwiched between those long jolting rides. Come in the van, your small car can't make it.

"Woodpecker still on tree. Mailbox still spilling. IRS report finished. No visitors over the long weekend. All I do is eat, although I've had fun editing a paper on Maine Least terns by a woman named Elizabeth Pierson. Do you know her? I don't. She telephoned me in Tucson, and by a miracle I was there. It is for *The Country Journal;* they print a lot of good environmental articles. I hope she gets it accepted; those birds need help.

"I know Spoff says bird names aren't capitalized (why not?) but after all the work I've done on Leasts I'd write them in inch-high letters if this machine could arrange it. Tell him to stop being such a purist. Besides, to capitalize or not is controversial. Look at all the writers who do it. I'm only an amateur, I don't have to follow rules."

February 27th, Tuesday. Continuation of above letter

"That was last week, this is this week, with marvelous weather. Still no birds so I am off to Sasabe to explore the outside world, exercise the car battery, buy eggs, a flashlight, new sneakers, send out mail, and replace the suet I left out overnight that someone took away along with my painfully constructed wire feeder. Same fellow that took the Bantam rooster, I'll bet. Juncos gone. Kinglets gone. Winter must be over."

February 28th. Letter to Hal Scott, President of Florida Audubon Society, a fellow bander

"In answer to your questions on bird life, I've been disappointed. Perhaps unreasonably, as the number of species banded, with more observed, compares with my winter listings in Florida. It's just that there all those hundreds of catbirds and jays and robins and buntings and redwings, and sporadic influxes of goldfinch, waxwings, and myrtle warblers produced a lot of action and kept me on my toes. One winter, running two nets a couple of hours a day when the Florida holly—which you probably call *Schinus terebinthifolia,* a beautiful weed tree by any name that may be the death of Florida (it is so poisonous and indestructible) was in fruit, I took 1,163 myrtles. Wow! (But the next year only six.) Nothing like that activity here. I run eleven nets all day and am lucky if I get four, or six total. Mostly repeats. Now that juncos and kinglets have left and the local residents have learned what traps and nets are I am discouragingly empty-handed. The road up is so rough I get few visitors.

"Deer and cattle congregate in the few shady places. I tried keeping them out with brush fences, but this didn't work; cattle weigh too much, deer run too fast. So I decided to try clothesline, which wouldn't work either but would keep me busy. Tramped down to my car yesterday with some hikers, also going out, and drove to the only two towns within twenty miles, Sasabe and Arivaca. Nice names. Maybe a dozen, or score, of buildings apiece. Each had a small general store but no clothesline, hamburger, flashlight, shoelaces—normal essentials, you might think. Returned only with eggs, and the first good head of lettuce I've had all winter. Must have come from Mexico—Sasabe is a border town. It had a gas station, a sandwich shop (closed), and a Customs office. Ninety-nine cents (the lettuce) and every leaf worth it. I am growing some of my own in my workshop-aviary-greenhouse porch. It is coming very well.

"On the way home I explored the side roads. There were only a couple and went endlessly and apparently aimlessly through dry, barren desert. Interesting but monotonous. I better understand why The Conservancy wanted to save the diversity of Thomas Canyon.

"The winter migrants are gone, spring ones not yet arrived, although a few warm days (at last and thank God, this has been the coldest winter on record) have bred swarms of flying insects. In the valley the shrikes were two by two on the power lines. Up here the verdin and Say's phoebes seem paired. The Cactus wrens have built a home by my car from Kleenex they found on a campsite. Anemones are in bloom but not as colorful as your hibiscus. Verbena flowers in damp places all around the Ranch, but I have seen hummingbirds only twice—an adult male Anna's, and a female that would be a migrant no matter which of two similar species it was. Mountain birds aren't accustomed to feeders but the jays—Mexican, not your Florida Scrub (I've read these can be here but seen none)—finally caught on to free food, and the Gila woodpecker comes for peanut butter I slather on a tree. It leaves a little in the crevices for a Bewick's wren.

"That's enough to read. Thank you for asking. Which Florida politicians are you trying to convince of what?

February 28th. Evening, after a trip to Sasabe and Arivaca

When finally I climb through the horse bars, clutching a head of lettuce, and go to put it in the fridge at the Big House where I now have to keep perishables because mine isn't cold enough, the house key isn't on its nail. It has lived there ever since my arrival. I search everywhere—in pockets, my banding box, inside the cabin, outside. . . . I am a disorderly woman, always setting things down to put away later. I can't find it anywhere. Oh well—there is one for emergency by the door of the second floor. Ian showed it to me, laughing, hung on a slat on the garden fence in plain sight of anyone wishing to break in. Rancher and Peggy were here the other day; perhaps they accidentally went off with mine? As they left Peggy asked if I knew about that emergency one. She started to take me up the steps to show me, but Big Egotist, always knowing more than anybody else, I had to say: "I *know*. Never mind." So she didn't.

Now when I look I can't find it. The peacocks watch with supercilious expressions from their beds in the ivy. Have they pecked it off its hook, thinking it a toy for their pleasure? I paw through the leaves by the fence. I rake. I use a flashlight, hoping the rusty metal may shine. Those darned birds! Defeated, I circle the house, hunting a window that is unlocked, and find one. When I have pried it open with a screwdriver and boards it sticks. To get inside I must inch backward, squirming on my tummy, and drop down onto a window seat. I fetch milk, mayonnaise, leftover chicken, set them outside, and reverse. When supper has been made and eaten I carry everything back, squirming in and out again. This is going to restrict my eating!

Otherwise all is serene.

March 2nd

Drowsy in the half dark of 6:30 A.M. I am aware of a silence, an odd quality of air that goes back into childhood winters. I can't identify it. Turning my head, I am astonished to see a white world. Deep snow lies on the tropical bamboo and agaves, on the stone wall, on the roofs of the ramshackle chicken coop and dog houses and other abandonments of past living. On vines and mesquite branches as far as I can see—SNOW! I can't see far, only to the nearest hill. Beyond everything is blotted out—to the Peak by a creamy white sky, down Canyon by a sullen purple. A thin sifting of flakes is still falling. March is coming in like a lion. The Papago gods are showing off.

Yesterday, lured—deceived—by four days of balmy blue "typical Arizona weather," I had planned to climb the ridges that mount fold on fold up by the sheer cliff of the Peak, and photograph. But the day had turned gray; by afternoon the wind was hard. Although with the turning of our planet it is not dark now until nearly seven, my lamp was lit long before that, along with a fire in the stove for cheer. In the night I heard rain dripping onto the metal seed can, a sound become so unaccustomed that I got up to see if I had left a faucet dripping. Now the world is blocked off, silent in white.

I dress and scatter breakfast for the peacocks. They have again knocked down the redwood benches on the Big House porch that Herman carefully upends for cleanliness. In bad weather do they always displace these, and huddle on them because wood is kinder to their feet than wet cement? Or is it because their pea heads are then higher under the porch roof, out of the rain? WHY are peacocks up here in the snow anyway? There is a half inch of water in the rain gauge, under a snowy crust.

At 8:30 I celebrate by eating rice cakes and that delicious bacon of Herman's I snitched from the Big House because it was spoiling. I watch a Bewick's wren pick its way up the tree trunk outside the window to the peanut butter. It may be that this recently discovered source of protein is keeping my 5.5-gram friends alive in these last harsh days of winter. Two wear bands, I see them often. They do not sing like their ubiquitous cousins, the Canyon wrens, which all day hop in and out of the stone walls and rafters, and occasionally inside my cabin. For black widow spiders, I hope. A Hermit thrush is fluffed under a snowy bush, its supply of pyracantha berries long gone. Rancher's Wife brought me a sack of frozen pomegranates on their last trip. I stamp on these, staining the cement with red juice, and set the halves in a sotol agave where a small bird can get at them, but perhaps not the peacocks, who also love them. It is snowing again, thinly, wind blowing it in every direction.

March 3rd. The Birthday of our Firstborn

I commemorate the above in this Sun Belt state—fatest growing mecca of senior citizens, its water table rapidly sinking, smog hiding its mountains—by breaking ice in the peacocks' water pans, and by photographing Baboquivari in snowy splendor. I throw birdseed with a lavish hand for my fellow creatures, at the end of their winter's endurance. The peacocks appreciate this. It is the sweet-singing thrush I am looking for—sheltered where in the inclement night? Inside the Banding Office, crept in to avoid the wind, a Canyon wren greets me. Outside, nets sagging with frozen snow will have fallen, or be full of cat's claw, oak leaves, and branches, as easy to handle as porcupines. They had been furled tightly but they and I will be in trouble.

"Done," in the afternoon, "my usual chores." A woman always has chores of sweeping and cleaning, or at least, in the phrase of my Vermont aunt, redding up. Here, along with care of the nets, I shovel ashes, clean lamps and candles, check batteries, camera and recorder, sort again through the carton on the floor to see which unmet obligations need my last few stamps. Good occupation for a cold and snowy day. At supper time I pour a glass of sherry.

When the day is dreary and I have tracked peacock shit again in on Gene's rug I often wonder: what am I doing here on this mountain, feeding peacocks? Then I think—I make myself think—where would I rather be? Back in that Boston hospital cradling that red and marvelous baby? OH, YES! In those days "the world was wide as the sky is wide" and Vincent

Millay was my favorite author. I pour a second sherry and look back across the years. I hear the resonant voice of the rector of our church. In my teens those words rolling over me had music but little meaning. But I have learned. . . . "For everything there is a season. A time to plant . . . a time to mourn. A time to embrace and a time to refrain from embracing; a time to seek . . . and a time to cast away. A time to keep silence. A time to love . . . and a time for peace. A time for every purpose under heaven."

Even if I don't know what this last is. That hospital, that baby, his father with arms full of flowers, are a world away in time. Rather than here would I prefer to be manning a desk at some eleemosynary institution? Teaching Scouts, raising funds for an orchestra, going to meetings and lunches given because some other woman has the need to keep busy? Taking craft courses on Cape Cod? Rushing about the city in taxis, hurrying to catch planes as our successful, fashionable business daughter does? My problem is, of course, that I lack someone to share living with; someone who will laugh, but care when I clobber myself with a hammer; who will take the car for service. Someone to cook for, and care for. A thirty-six-year habit is hard to discard.

But I have listened to too many women in second marriages envy me my independence. There are worse things than loneliness. Widows haven't many options, not at my age. Contentment is not the same as happiness, but it is a very solid state. When the sun is shining and I am handling a new bird I consider I am the luckiest widow in the world. I set my glass down. Back to work.

March 4th. Letter to the Spoffords

"You mean you don't have a bed available in all of April???!!
You *will* keep reporting exotic birds so the world arrives at
your door by busloads.

"I need to see Guadalupe Canyon. Bill is talking of sending
me there to work. Next year. It is right on the Mexican border, the birds would be more varied, and abundant. But it is
open and may be too windy. Also there may be a problem of
living quarters over a period of time. So I want to look at it,
and talk with the Fish & Wildlife people there, to judge if
they would take me in. I looked at a map the other day when
it was snowing and found it is next door to your shopping
town of Douglas. We could meet for lunches, or you could
drive out—what is another twenty miles when you have already
been sixty? I thought: 'Ha! Maybe the Spoffs will let me spend
the night. I can see the Canyon the next day and be back in
time for rum and Roast Road-runner and Hummingbird
Tongues for dinner, and spend a second night so as to scrum-
ple your sheets properly.'

"As I have two sets of relatives coming soon (they say), I
was thinking in terms of April. Oh, well—if any of those

migrant birds I am promised show up I'll need to be here, nose to grindstone. I've an Audubon Board Meeting in Ohio the end of that month, then I pack and return East. Come help?

"Rancher and the Road Man are here for lunch. They promise to fix the road so I can drive to my very doorstep. Imagine! Larry the skinny botanist is here. At forty-one he has gone back to school. Works as a waiter; they can't feed him much. I loaned him your copy of *The Journey Home;* he seems responsible. He staggered in with high blood pressure and ten pounds of mail. I haven't answered the last batch yet.

"Local snow melted; sun hot; spirits good. Been mending nets. There is the peacock-hole net, the cow-hole net, the fallen oak-branch net; and the net that collapsed with snow and ice and spent a day solidifying in green algae in a flooded wash. Tedious but peaceful work. Rancher is here and will mail this. That's not my hanky you sent, I use Kleenex. The Cactus wrens make nests with it. I *did* get a typewriter, as you requested. My sister borrowed one for me, it arrived broken. You will have to keep on struggling with my hen tracks (peahen tracks). Sorry."

March 7th, I think

The way I figure this is that two days ago I caught a Hutton's vireo, a new bird for my life list. (New to William Hutton, too, who collected and described it first at Monterey, California sometime in 1847–48; not much is known about Hutton. I was in Monterey three weeks ago, but I didn't see one. Or know enough to look.) My records for U.S. Fish & Wildlife are always correct—well, within a day or two. If I am excited, or take only one or two birds, or if it has rained, sometimes I forget to list the date and my sheets get a little out of whack. You would think the Tucson radio would have the courtesy, along with their morning weather and news bulletins, to give the day and date, but all they give is the time. I *know* the time, more or less. My watch with its sweep hand runs well if I wind it, but I forget. I need a watch so I will run nets at regular intervals. I have a heavy, round, bedside clock that goes with me to all my homes. It is glass so from the back I see its mechanism ticking my life away. It is inscribed to Brad's grandfather, John C. Bradley. Date 1912. Old J. C. was a

courteous, soft-spoken executive who answered his own door-
bell and approved of me because I ate oatmeal for breakfast in
addition to the ham and eggs and toast and honey and whatever else a country woman served us, and I helped her churn
our butter. He had a poor opinion of my taste in radio music,
though, and switched the knob irritably to political news. The
Vermont road he lived on bears his name (unless the town has
changed it to River Road again). I plan to send his great-great-
grandson namesake up to see someday, and to fish in the Bat-
tenkill with one of J.C.'s trout flies I still keep. They are almost
as old as that first Hutton's vireo. I plan a lot of things that
don't necessarily happen, doesn't everybody?

I plan to wind old J.C.'s clock every Sunday, too, only I
forget. If I absolutely *had* to know the time, to check on Tucson's breathy, hurrying voice, I could trot down to my car
where the clock is always correct. Why does it seem necessary,
more civilized, to know exactly what time it is? Are we so
afraid of getting lost, adrift in frightening space?

The phoebes use last year's nest on the rafter by the door of the Big House as a roost. They fly off every time I go up to the fridge there for eggs or lettuce or a spot of milk, or whatever. My own fridge won't even make ice after freezing everything solid, even half gallons of milk, all winter! It isn't the distance, it is the aggravation. I always forget something and have to traipse back. Herman and Larry and Peggy keep food there too, which they may need when they come. I hesitate to poach, though I am often tempted, the shelves are so crowded.

At night I need a flashlight to see what I am rummaging for. As I recross the porch I flick my beam on the phoebes, saying Goodnight. They sit tight in the dark, but their eyes shine alertly, watching me. We are familiars.

Undated letter to Molly at Harvard

"Pay no attention to my complaints, I love it here.

"We all live on several levels. While I was grumbling to you about that church group of youngsters who had left their trash around, threw cans and bottles into the burning barrels so I had to dig them out, I did not tell you how at the same time I was listening to the Cactus wren orating on his bush to the wind and the peacocks that rustle in the bamboo by those barrels; how I was trying to identify small plants as I wheeled our spavined barrow to the dump, rejoicing as always at the clarity of air between me and Baboquivari. My eyes and spirit lift to that great rectangle every time I step outside. I take for granted the jays that whoop into the tree by the Big House in flashes of blue light the way you take for granted the snarl and smell of traffic, the police sirens, and hurrying crush of people in Harvard Square. I imagine that when you jog to Weld Boathouse for crew practice, on one level you think of the pebble in your sneaker, a paper you must type, while on another you are seeing the glint of the sun on the river, the dappled shade of those old plane trees that line its bank. At your age you live on an emotional level, too, and will be remembering the young man who saw you home last night, and his *abrazo*. I have covered over that level, it is easier for me.

"But when you jog along that path under those trees, by where the Cowley Fathers live—are they still there, or did the Kennedy School of Government displace them, as it did the old street car barns?—look sharp. I am wheeling my baby along that same path, watching light shift on the same water where the oarsmen of fifty years ago stroked by. Not many women in my day! Like you I learned to manage a wherry, and then a "comp" the year I went to Summer School. When you cross Anderson Bridge there goes your grandfather, on his way to class at Business School. Or a merry group of us on football Saturdays, marching with the bands and balloons and banners, ducking and laughing among laggards, getting separated in the crush. Coonskin coats. Hip flasks. Right out of Scott Fitzgerald, but for real. Your father walked that Bridge, too, and your great grandfather, if it was built in his day. Your Aunt Amanda went to Summer School there one year, and our dog Tappy. Links in a chain, generation after generation.

"What I am saying, only as usual I get off the subject, is that it isn't the learning to cook and change diapers, the problems I remember now, but the river, the color and jostle and happiness of those Saturdays, the trying to pitch an apple core down the Cowley Fathers' chimney from our balcony. When I write you about my small discomforts (everyone has them) they are only dust on the shining web of the beauty here, the peace.

"You'd be surprised how much beer is drunk on a Religious Retreat! Unless a cowboy was here in my absence. And did you know that the Cambridge Street Dept. once tried to cut down those fine old trees to widen Memorial Drive? After my day, before yours. Little girls and their mothers climbed up in the branches, tied themselves in, and prevented it. That for commercialism and the automobile!

March 8th

I have done little these past two days but mend nets. A peaceful occupation, no duller than addressing envelopes in Buffalo, reviewing papers in D. C., or making calamondin marmalade in Florida. A warm breeze stirs the oak leaves, the sun is hot. Jays chatter across the Creek, keeping each other in touch.

How can there be so many holes? The small ones would be where clutching claws could not be loosened, or where in my impatience I broke a strand to free a wing caught too tightly. The biggest is from a cow. The peacocks learned about nets and now go around them, but they were slow learners. Here is a tear not present at 7:00 A. M., jeering at me now at 9:00. A deer? Too big, too low for a hawk. Too big, too high for a ground squirrel. I weave patiently. Every half hour I make rounds, but the other nets hang empty. A pair of verdin are nest-building on the route. I leave them strands of yellow wool, and mark the place with a torn Kleenex. Shortly these are gone. I glimpse the wool inside their spiny cave of thorn twigs, the Kleenex somehow reduced to an unrecognizable gray fluff that could as easily be cobwebs. I leave them more. A Say's phoebe, one from the pair at last year's nest on the Big House porch, flies low after a bug, then veers up and over my snaring net at the last moment. Eyes keen enough to discern minute flying insects are hardly blind to a dark nylon web. Nets, I feel, catch only careless birds in a hurry.

I took my first catch ever of a poor-will this morning, putting it in a paper bag while I fetched my camera. Its larger cousins, the whip-poor-wills and chuck-wills-widows I took in Florida, were always dazed by sunlight and lay quietly on the ground while I photographed them, so I prepared a clear setting in the garden and confidently set this smaller relative on it. Off it flew, with some choice, softly muttered remarks. For several years I banded more whips and chucks than any other bander in the country. Don't get excited. My high on chucks was only six, one fall. Whips were more common. They used to perch on my net poles at night, hunting. In my flashlight their eyes shone like rubies.

March 9th

I am going Outside. It's hard on the VW, but my flagging
spirits need to be jacked up. People get queer when they live
alone, it is said. How will I know? My children have always
thought me odd. What am I proving, taking two birds a day?
Bill and Alice are having cocktails before an Important Dinner
(I'll learn what when I get there). If I leave early I can be in
town by eleven, plenty of time for errands and telephoning
and sitting around laughing and hearing the news, for making
cocktail dips for Alice to thank her for her generous care of
me.

My polite clothes are in her guest closet. You might think
that for one night all I would need to take would be a toothbrush and nightgown; I can eat a swift breakfast and be gone,
right? Wrong. First I must empty the trash, so the mice won't
come hunting. (They will, anyway. Hunting, they have
knocked off my handsome daughter-given owl plate, breaking
it in a dozen pieces.) Never go anywhere without food. I crawl
backward through that window at the Big House to get sandwich makings, forget to fill my thermos with the last of the

real milk, decide against a second crawl. This window bit is getting me down, I can drink water. The outgoing mail and papers to be photocopied fill a tote bag. A raincoat—it looks like rain. If I don't hurry I won't make it dry to the car. A sweater, against unpredictable Arizona weather. City shoes, the insulated bag to bring perishables back in. By the time I have finished, both packs are full. I hang my binoculars around my neck and set off, late and whining, sacks banging against my back. A gray day, lowering down canyon. Two miles later inside my car it is 85 degrees and bright sun.

March 11th. Postcard to Amanda

"There must be a hundred javelina hunters in campers and trucks settled in on the road, right up to the Ranch gate. I am busy making a huge sign—pink is the only paint I find—saying PRIVATE, to add to the five NO HUNTING ones they can't seem to read already on the gate. I may be shot dead any time. A javelina is a peccary, does that help you? Hurry with that long letter you keep advertising. How do you like your new job?"

March 10th. Return from Tucson. March 10th is the day before the 11th. I know.

Javelina Season has opened. Sunday hunters are parked along the highway, weighing stations are set up. At my turnoff a tin can hangs from a red ribbon. At the first gate pink strands of wool proclaim THIS WAY. As I maneuver the ruts of the single-lane, desert road, trucks and jeeps send dust swirling as they barrel toward me. No Rule of the Sea here, where small craft have the right of way. Not in this country! They come straight at me, making me mad enough so that after the third one I hold course and *they* have to swerve into the thorn bushes. It took me a while in Washington to learn to go through doors first, as the wife of an Assistant Secretary. Under pressure the haughty habit returns.

On the second gate is a blue streamer; a pretty color so I let it be as I fasten the chain. I don't feel as kindly toward the fuschia one on the next, we are approaching my home. Oh well—I am lucky to live in this scenic valley every day, let city folk have their weekend fun. I pass small clusters of campers, in some places villages of them, pulled off into the few open flat areas. One Big Stupid has set up his tent and his family in a wash, careless of flash floods that can originate fifty miles away, swirl down unannounced. I see few women or children, though—mostly just men lounging in deck chairs, drinking.

"You'll break yer car," one calls derisively, waving a beer can at me. "You'll never make it."

I stare him down. "I live here," comes in my coldest New England tone, instead of "Thanks." He looked startled.

Fortunately I am out of his sight when an ominous scraping of metal slows me. I just might *not* make it, I realize, backing off a boulder. All these trucks coming in have worn the ruts deep, the crown of the road steadily gives me trouble. I lurch back and forth, taking advantage of the VW's narrower width.

At last the nest of the Cactus wren, a streamer of Kleenex its signal to me as colored wool has been to the hunters. Just beyond is my parking slot. I am weary.

SOMEONE ELSE IS IN IT! In MY slot!! I am outraged. Cranky from the difficult drive, from the invasion of my privacy by these people who may be looking for javelina but will not hesitate to poach on deer and quail if they see them—so that was why those two paunchy men asked me about quail the other day? They were surprised to find me at the Ranch. They obviously weren't hikers—"just looking around." They didn't stay.

I back the car, turning and twisting, trying to fit off the road first here, then there, scratching paint on branches, crashing the rear window against an unseen mesquite. I never was a skillful backer.

A horn interrupts my angry concentration, a truck lurching uphill from the ford. Rancher Brother, bless him, on his way out! Always courteous, always concerned for me. I'm sure he was in a hurry, but couldn't he drive me, and all that stuff I would otherwise have to lug, bumping on my shoulders, shifting in my sweaty hands, the rest of the way? Could he! I scramble hastily into his truck, I shouldn't delay him, he lives 150 miles away. But not until my sacks are set at the cabin, the keys to the Big House found—At Last! The peacocks HAD knocked the emergency set off the fence, Peggy HAD hung the other on a different nail (her nail), would he leave me. I find his spurs later by the big chair where he rests after riding and rub them for him. With Ajax, my supplies don't run to silver polish.

Learning I would be gone over the weekend he had driven up to guard the Ranch. He tells me he had to evict one rough and burly group from the field inside our gate. That gate has five signs on it, from the big THE NATURE CONSERVANCY one to my small but very government-official U.S. Fish & Wildlife Service. But there was none reading PRIVATE PROPERTY, the evictees had grumbled, how were they to know they shouldn't come through? I remedied this the next morning. When I went to fasten it, and photograph my art, two new camping vehicles were set up fifty feet away. I begin to see why Rancher and Rancher Brother are pleased to have me living here.

They haven't said much to explain their frequent thanks for my being willing to stay. (Being willing! It is heaven, in its fashion.) Maybe they are afraid to frighten me. In the beginning both had urged me to keep a dog. On his first trip Rancher brought a liver-colored hound with yellow eyes, on loan. Hound and I regarded each other with mutual suspicion.

"Why?" I had asked them both. "*Why* do I need a dog?"

Both had fudged their replies. To keep away varmints. For company, I would be lonely (with all those peacocks underfoot?). The nearest they came to what must have been on their minds was that a dog would bark if anyone came around.

I don't want a dog. I would become fond of it, I would have to feed it. Being a patsy I would bring it into my warm cabin at night. I couldn't leave it tied when I went Outside, I am unwilling to chain an animal. I refused their offers, only dimly aware there must be a reason for them.

So—Rancher Brother had had to evict, with unpleasantness, trespassers. Well, I might have been up to that. Poachers I hadn't really considered. But here in my mail is a newspaper clipping and photographs of a Golden eagle found dead along with a pile of dead coyotes, jackrabbits, and crows on state-leased land not too far from here.

There are only about a hundred nesting Goldens in all of Arizona. Occasionally one soars past the Peak, floats over the Ranch, and disappears down the valley. On a dead tree below the Rhyolite Cliffs I once saw two perched together, an adult and an immature. Ian reported one up there, too. Rancher says there used to be a nest. This one in the clipping had been shot in the head. The coyotes had been skinned. There was a big pile of them, and a bigger one of rabbits. The carcasses were heaped together beside shotgun shells and two traps. Why? Why had they been left? What were the traps to catch? Eagle feathers sell for fifty dollars apiece on the black market. A five-thousand-dollar fine and a year in jail are the penalty for killing one, but who is to know?

While I see coyote scat every day I have not yet seen the animal, to my disappointment. They used to be common. If they are a threat to crops or to a rancher's property they can be shot, and obviously are, threat or not. The result is a population explosion of jackrabbits, equally damaging. The balances of nature are finely tuned. We are only beginning to understand how finely. Each link in the chain leads to another, and sooner or later they all lead to man's interests, including the health of his harvests. The effects of greed can be seen in our dust bowls; in our mountains stripped, eroded, mined, and abandoned; in our falling water tables; in the desolate cliffs of tailings along these Arizona roads, in the mounds of old cars and junk piled along rivers in a futile effort to save flood plains—and the expensive homes built on them.

If I had a gun I would sure enough use it on anyone I saw shooting an eagle. I'm a poor shot. I needn't be afraid of hitting the miscreant, but I sure enough would let fly with it. I suppose the thought of poachers coming up the road should sober me, as I now see it did Rancher. Instead it just makes me mad. There would have to be something comic in the sight of a woman my size and age berating trespassers on our property. I'm glad it hasn't happened. Just that big sign in pink paint proclaiming PRIVATE.

March 12th

I took a chilled, bewildered, Black-chinned hummingbird out
of a net and held it in my lap for twenty minutes before breakfast, feeding it sugar syrup. I did one hummer in, I'm not
about to lose another. The female Black-chinned is "not safely
separable" from the female of another southwest species, the
three-inch Costa (which, surprisingly, is also found on islands
off Baja California.) These facts are according to my friend
and teacher Chan Robbins, co-author of *Birds of North America;*
and to Blake (Emmet Reid), whose *Birds of Mexico* I tugged
out here with all my other Mexican books, expecting to need
them daily.

To keep my mind off my own sugar syrup, caffeinated, not
yet poured, I consider the Frenchman who discovered this
feathered scrap in the Sierra Madre of Mexico. He was well
enough known to his peers to have had *Archilochus alexandri*
named for him, but has come down to us only as "Dr. Alexander." It surprises me—I think of them as fur people, not
bird people—how many species are named for the French. A

Frenchman, Lesson, named the Blue-throated hummingbird, *Lampornis clemenciae*, for his wife. He also named the Heloise's (or Bumblebee, found only in Mexico), but the books don't say for whom. Hmm. *Sasin* (Allen's hummingbird), on the other hand, is a Nootka Indian name.

I learn about nomenclature from *The Dictionary of American Bird Names,* written by Ernie Choate, a retired, tough, cantankerous school principal friend of mine. He researched his book for years, delving into Greek and Roman mythology, amassing marvelous tales, only to have the manuscript destroyed in a publisher's fire. Before he could put it together again a rival volume came out, scotched his glory, broke his heart. He was even more cantankerous after that.

Cuddled in my warm hand my patient revives. Its slender tubular tongue absorbs the caloried liquid first from my thumb, then from a bottle I hold to its bill. Its heartbeat becomes stronger. It exercises its wings tentatively, clinging to my finger perch with tiny, razor-sharp claws. It is a male. The purple stripe below his black throat flashes as he turns his head in the sun, drinks more deeply, looks all about for possible enemies, then zooms off. What enemies can hummingbirds have? Spider webs can entangle them, they have been found snared in cholla cactus. They weigh less than a dime—2.4 grams for this Black-chinned, to be exact.

Over coffee I look him up in *The Birds of Arizona,* which gets more thumbed every day. Black-chins, it tells me, Allan Phillips writing, are common in southern Arizona, nesting along rivers and streams, and in the olive trees of towns. They often feed like flycatchers, darting after insects instead of patronizing local flower delicatessens for bugs so small you and I wouldn't see them. (Phillips doesn't use this language.) As with many species, the male arrives first to scout out a summer territory for his lady. They may raise two broods, and even return to the same twig in the same branch in the same tree in successive years, which would make it easier for me to study them.

BUT—note the capital letters—they are "generally absent in deserts," and occur "from the middle of March, rarely earlier." So I am pleased to provide for the record my desert mountain locality, and beat that midmonth date by three days. Four—my breakfasting visitor must surely have spent the night by the Creek where I caught him. Unless he was up mighty early, shaking the dust of Mexico from those tiny feet.

(Note: I took four in the next few weeks, and saw others, but none after April 5th. Probably they were migrants flying the mountain route, attracted by that clump of sycamores over the ridge. There are always hatches of insects there now, and flycatchers and hummers.)

March, undated

Rancher and Peggy have been here. Sometimes they come with a son, sometimes with Herman, sometimes alone. Rancher takes a bucket of oats and goes off, calling the horses. What senses animals have! Those beasts, far off on the hills, out of my sight sometimes for days, smell the food and show up, willing to be led docilely into the corral where Rancher saddles them. Not always docile, Peggy stands by. Then Doug rides off to count cattle and look for sign of mountain lion. As a young man he led safaris and had considerable reputation as a White Hunter, but he has seen the state he loves change to such a degree—from overgrazing, development, the spreading ugliness of mining—that he has become an ardent protector of land and its wildlife. He has started a conservation group down by Nogales and invites me to a meeting of it. I tack its handsome poster on the Ranch door for visitors to read.

Peggy is of two minds on development. They live near—thirty miles in this fast-driving country is near—the retirement community of Green Valley. Once small and attractive, now huge with houses side by side on a suburban grid, more and more condominiums going in for the benefit of out-of-state operators, it offers a first-rate shopping mall. For a rancher's wife who has had to make do the hard way for many years, to spend a full day driving to Tucson to shop, this is a luxurious convenience.

Peggy is a hard worker. Before she even feeds her family she gets out the hose, washes the peacock droppings from her porch, sweeps vigorously, and sets to work pruning and planting in gardens she may not tend for another month. She would like me better, I think, if I did more of this, as well as keeping the peacocks from eating the new green iris shoots. I try, but they fly over fences, I fail. She always invites me to join their meals, but my peanut butter sandwich hour is earlier. She brings me fresh milk and lettuce, notes the herbs and petunias I have growing on the sunporch and the care I give her potted plants there. We have become friends. So far Rancher has found no indication of lions harassing his cattle, although a number of his cows crossed the fences in January when snow was deep. If cattle stray into Papago land, though, I understand they are gone for good.

March 13th

I have been searching ornithological journals for Arizona references for Gale Monson.

"Why are you doing that?" a visitor asked me disdainfully. "That's scut work."

I am a slow thinker. "Well, everything I do is scut work," I answered feebly. "I enjoy it."

I wish I weren't so meek! Why couldn't I have said I was proud to be doing anything that involved me with Gale Monson, an esteemed expert on Arizona's land and wildlife, that would help him? Why couldn't I have pointed out that leafing through journals full of information I could wish lodged in my head is pleasure, not labor?

I am thinking of this again this afternoon as I mend a net. Here I sit, on a rock at one end of the slippery nylon mesh, weaving, while at the other end one of Rancher's special hybrid Herefords tranquilly munches on new green grass. Doubtless the same animal responsible for the tear I am working on. We each tend to our own business, comfortable in the shade.

"Scut work." Spring housecleaning, which I did this morning with energy and pleasure, is scut work. Washing dishes, watering the flowers that a wing-loud hummingbird comes to,

chopping a net lane. Driving Brad to work all those years—
how I wish that scut work still existed! Driving children to
school, to dentists and music lessons, serving punch and cookies at basketball games and graduations, years and years of this
chauffeuring, what was that but scut work? Someone has to
gas the car, write the checks, answer the phone, run meetings,
shovel snow, plant pansies, spread manure, do the mending.
It is attitude, not labor, that makes scut work. It's what you
build with—people, a home, research. Taking eagle and heron
censuses was scut work really, flying in a small hot plane over
Everglades National Park, secretarial work fobbed off on me
by a busy biologist. Netting those tropical birds for Don Eck-
elberry, getting bitten, scratched, bone-weary; measuring them
for Richard ffrench's *Bird Guide:* making bird skins in Ecuador
and British Honduras in dim light after a muddy day in the
field was scut work done for my betters, but what a glorious
life it gave me! Here I am now, in the warm Arizona sun under
an incredibly blue sky listening to a cow munch, the remnant
Creek murmur, a light breeze in the oak leaves above me, a
bird tentatively proclaiming Spring nearby. I'm mending,
which is scut work, but I surely don't feel downtrodden!

Finished, I contemplate that heavy white cow, which con-
templates me, as do her fourteen companions arrived through
the mesquite. Obviously they desire the shade under our tree.
Deer run through this hollow, too. Since barriers I erected
have been ineffective I will move my nets to the other side of
the cattle fence. I don't really mind taking down this net; I
keep stumbling in the jumble of rocks and cactus under it,
and with a few more hot days it may be rattlesnake area. There
are seventeen kinds of rattlesnakes in Arizona. I try to ignore
this.

It has been a pleasant walk out here, though, through the

corral gates, by the verdin building their thorny nest, along the trail leading to the Peak. I'll miss it. Where the trail turns toward the saddle a hill rises steeply. I want to climb there some day. The bear went over the mountain . . .

I gather up scissors, thread, poles, guy ropes, the mended net and go off to see who may have flown elsewhere and be awaiting release. Running nets all day is often scut work, particularly when I am weary, or bored with no results. Not to mention the record keeping, the analyses, the typing by lamplight. (I finally bought a typewriter.) But it adds up eventually to research, however minuscule. Something that needs doing that no one else is available to do. I wonder what that disdainful visitor does with *her* time?

March 14th

I now see hummingbirds daily at my feeders. Anna's and Black-chinned and others, they fly too fast to identify, the sun has to shine on them at just the right angle to bring out their iridescent colors. Someone at night is emptying the jars of sugar water I put out in the hope tanagers and orioles will find them. A Black-headed grosbeak did the other day, but the big stupid banged at the glass sides instead of dipping in from the top, he didn't stay.

I slept poorly last night. Moonlight pouring across my pillow tempted me to keep twisting my head to admire the ridges outlined against a bright sky. But more than that, I had left some nets open. Predators are abroad at night, and I smelled skunk. Now that it is warm the windows by my bedhead are open—the only ones I *can* open, if my papers are not to blow all about the room. (Some people stack their papers neatly in boxes, I keep telling myself; uselessly.) I find coyote scat daily. Are the peacocks roosting at a distance instead of by the barn to evade a bobcat, or the fox? I left only the highest tier of my nets open, out of animal reach, but still I worry.

I wouldn't leave them open at all but my Whiskered owl has been questioned. I didn't know enough, when this small angry creature stabbed grimly into my hand to check—I told you this—that inner web of the outer wing feather. If this is the chief difference between it and the Screech owl no wonder they can be told apart in the field only by their voices! My catch wasn't singing to me that morning, just snapping. So I need to snare him again. Restless, I reach for the flashlight and go out on a security check.

Owls are night fliers. I suppose they *do* fly at midnight, and in Florida I often got up to make sure none had and were caught, but I took them only at dusk and dawn.

In these mountains the stars are glorious. The nearest lights are at Kitts Peak thirty miles north. I have seen stars like this only in the Dry Tortugas in the Gulf of Mexico, where a group of us used to go each spring to band thousands of Sooty tern; and at Brad's fishing camp, deep in the Canadian woods. The stars there were so bright in September that I could paddle my canoe by their light into a mysterious swamp behind our cabin. And was totally unnerved one night when a beaver slapped his tail and dove from a log not two feet behind me. I thought it was at least a bear, or a moose, but starlight showed only ripples in the black water. We often saw moose in that swamp, and once a bear placidly ate raspberries outside our bedroom window. Brad had me wear a shrill Scout whistle when I went hiking alone.

If I had a whistle here, who would hear? Tonight moonlight

is bright over the hills. Not even a peacock's hoohaw breaks the silence. I can see my usual paths well, my feet have learned the obstacles, but I use my flashlight. It is warm enough for those rattlesnakes Bill advertises to have emerged. They are supposed to seek heat-gathering paths at night. I have seen no snakes at all. Yet.

Crossing the boulders of the Creek I wish I had a *searchlight*. I won't leave this net open again. What a ninny to have put one on the far side of this broad jumble where rocks slip and turn under my feet even in the daytime! I am never entirely sure, if I have forgotten to take my pills (I hate pills), that my gimpy hip is going to balance me. But this is a different habitat, tempting. An old road runs into a clearing shaded by oaks. I will use the cow-torn mended net, though, until I make sure deer do not bounce through the opening. Washed out by last June's cloudburst the road stops abruptly at a four-foot drop to the Creek. Difficult to climb. No owl.

March 15th

Variously known as the Ides of March, Income Tax Day, or, to the ancient Romans, as the festival Hilaria, whose undoubtedly rowdy merriment has come down to us in our word "hilarious."

Out again before light. No owl. The peacocks are up with me. What these birds find, picking in the weeds and dirt, to sustain their bulk, grow those flashy tail feathers, I can't guess. I feed them grain morning and night, what do they live on when no one is here? They eat every kernel I scatter for the smaller birds, hoping to bring these to my window. They have stripped the buds from the jonquils and iris in the abandoned gardens. Peggy is furious. It isn't *my* fault! They snuggle half the day where the ivy is thick (and that key hung). I strung a pot of red petunias on the porch for hummingbirds, who came right to it. Half an hour later a peahen was leaning from the roof, pulling out the blossoms. Damnable creatures.

They are scenic, though. Mating season is coming. Royal now has a four-foot, gorgeous, iridescent tail, of emerald brilliance, and gold.

> A royal train,
> Lord,
> more scintillating
> than jewelled enamel.
> Look,
> now I spread it in a wheel.

De Gasztold wrote of her peacock, obviously as arrogant as my Primero,

> I must say I derive
> some satisfaction
> from my good looks.
> My feathers
> are sown with eyes
> admiring themselves.

Primero keeps chasing Male Number 2, establishing dominance. Segundo's tail is only half as long so he is more nimble at running, escaping his tormentor behind bushes and piles of old lumber. Around and around they go until both are exhausted. A few minutes later I see them feeding placidly together. Segundo chases Tercero, who has almost no tail at all, the women would never give him a glance. In December I had thought there were two cocks only. As winter progressed the combs on some of the "hens" turned blue and their breasts began to show color. Apparently these were last summer's hatch, which are just beginning to show sex characteristics.

The skinny white one, sometimes outcast, sometimes protected by a hen, Rancher says had a father that was a cross between a game cock and a Bantam. He says he knows this positively, who am I to dispute him? Joe Hickey, who, between his ornithological accomplishments, first proved the evils of DDT, has suggested I study these creatures. No work has been done on feral peacocks, he says. Notebook at the ready, I have tried. But as far as I can determine their displays of raised tails and shaking feathers occur without rhyme or reason as both threats and protective behavior, to trucks, jeeps, people, cats, each other and especially to me, who feeds them. Sorry, Joe.

The Canyon wrens are early up, hunting in the brush piles and stonewall, singing. Verbena is blooming in a sheet all down the hill where the water tank overflows, and a wide-faced flower, an oenothera. There are deer tracks between them.

Yesterday Alice's mother brought me two blue hen's eggs from Delaware, and some huge mushrooms. What a sybaritic life I lead! (From time to time.) I decide to eat all of them for breakfast on the excuse that I need a lot of protein at this altitude (and am tired of peanuts and raisins). How often do you get blue eggs? I set bread toasting in the iron skillet (the best system I have found) and cut the pink grapefruit that was Alice's generous gift.

In spite of the difficult road, people come and go. Children dabble their feet in the waterfalls and pools of the drying Creek. Little boys fly kites that come to grief (both) in cat's claw and prickly pear cactus, amid the curses of parents who must retrieve them. Fathers climb the ridges, grandparents soak up the sun. Birdwatchers are full of questions I can't answer, but helpful with the nomenclature of butterflies and plants. They all bring a taste of the world outside. One very small, rubbery, and determined miss had finally to be leashed with a rope to make sure of her whereabouts.

March 16th

I didn't feed the peacocks this morning, I was busy feeding sugar syrup to another hummingbird. It is warm, there are lots of insects, I threw out grain for them last evening. Besides, they have eaten all the flowers they can stretch to off the small apricot tree by the outhouse. These were a tangible, treasured sign of real Spring, a good bit more impressive than anemones and ground squirrels. I am always stepping in peacock dung. They knock my traps over, even off the branches Ian nailed these to. At nine o'clock I am nursing my spirit with well-deserved pancakes and coffee, having found nothing but the hummer on my rounds. I decide spring migration is like road repair—everyone talks about it, enthusiastically promises it, but nothing happens.

So what happens as I am peacefully reading *The Smithsonian* and sopping up maple syrup from snowy New Hampshire? Outside each window, on the stovepipe here, grouped on top of the abandoned refrigerator by the shower there, on the trash can of grain, on the chair of the porch, clamber these idiot birds, peering in every window at me; whining, demanding to know What Am I Doing, Why Haven't I Fed Them, When Am I Coming Out? I must say they have become gorgeously beautiful, and this is a rare recognition that I exist. A communication.

March 17th, St. Patrick's Day, when there will be a great, traffic-clogging parade in Boston

This is also the date that visually night and day are equally divided, although the true solstice is not for four more days. Atmospheric refraction makes the sun appear to be rising and setting over the horizon when actually it isn't. In Florida I could verify this observation, looking out over tomato flatlands; here the ridges block my vision. But the knowledge warms my bones and cheers me.

I sit at the window coddling a foot I ran a Barrel Cactus spine into, going out barefoot before breakfast to fill a feeder an Anna's hummingbird was buzzing at. Two towhees, of two kinds—Brown and Spotted; a Hermit thrush; a thrasher and a few juncos that haven't yet migrated are foraging in view, hunting for anything the ground squirrel may have left. Squirrel, or squirrels? I never see but one, but then, I never see but one Hermit thrush. They don't climb—the squirrels—so they don't take the peanut butter I smear on a tree for a lone woodpecker (one? more?) and the Bewick's wrens. I *do* see two of these.

Down valley the ocotillo is greening. By the outhouse the bridal white of the apricot tree had a curtain of bees around it for days. Then the curtain moved to a tree in the laundry yard that is sprouting leaves and blossoms. An ash? Winter at last is over.

Only at the moment it is hailing.

March 19th

The brown horse walked through my net across the Creek, the one I had such hopes for, that caught a flicker immediately in spite of its large deer tear. I saw my equine friend dragging the pole up the hill with tangled hoofs. I should have known that road would be used by someone, but I am disgruntled. To compensate me on this raw gray day, too cold to net, nothing attractive to do, through the horse bars laughing and singing comes a column of students from Mike and Diane Cohen's Trailside School of Vermont. Now operating under aegis of the National Audubon Society, the Cohens teach college courses and the art of living with others by driving their pupils about the United States in a bus. They study our country first-hand, talking and sometimes working with the men and women who farm, mine, build dams and sewage systems, operate industries of every sort. They see in operation archaeology, Indian tribes, river-running, construction, forestry, manufacturing, learning to a degree never attained by reading books. They learn to live in amicable relationship, to handle their marketing, cleanliness, diet, jealousies, and adolescent hangups without the strictures of formal classrooms and parental dos and don'ts. They come out of it, necessarily, strong individuals able to cope with life.

For years they have stopped by my cottage in South Florida for a morning of question and answer, of small birds studied in the hand. They listened to the rapid heartbeats, saw differences in plumages, learned about the role of birds in our environment, their ecology. More important, they learned a respect for creatures different from themselves, with senses and abilities often keener than theirs.

How have they located me? Mike laughs. The bus had to

be left far down canyon, they have hiked in, each one bringing me a big orange or grapefruit—they fill a table with such bounty. To reward them I am able to produce little, alas—no birds in the hand, a clouded mountain, a cold wind, I teach as best I can with no birds to help. Then, exploring, we examine a mountain water system, the erosive results of flash floods. We pick our way across the Creek and follow that old road where the horse downed my net. I find—what have I been doing all winter?—that it leads to Sycamore Creek and the wide bend where the grove and that old hawk's nest is—an easy run over a hill commanding a terrific view down valley. Why has Rancher not told me about this? Nets would be distant, but the horse path is easy and open, the habitat looks promising. Three of the students help fetch my equipment and set it up, learning patience, why I demand the job be done properly.

In our absence the others build a sturdy flight of rock steps up the bank I have been climbing on my knees—a marvelous gift that will save me many any irritating detour. I don't have time for detours! Scott and Liz and six-year-old Barbara Anne, with Bill as engineer, built me a similar one last month, further up the Creek by an island I had planned to clear for netting. But after falling on the rocks en route several times, and eyeing the heavy tree trunks and brush I would have to move, I abandoned that location. I test each solid step of this new gift, beaming, the masons also beaming at my delight. They then thank me—what have I done for them?—crawl through the horse bars and go off, laughing and singing as they came, to see Kitts Peak and dance, tonight, at an Indian campground. Bless their generous hearts, and the Cohens. What a lift to my week! I forget how alone I am, how dreary a gray day can be.

March 21st

The Spring, or Vernal Solstice, when the sun rises precisely east, the day that actually divides our day into two equal parts. If you operate by calendar and not by what is going on outside your window. What sun? Vernal is the more evocative adjective. I can use a bit of evoking. Rain and drizzle, hail and wind.

I stoked the stove. Worked on statistics for the winter quarter. Done my indoor chores muttering a rhyme I learned from Helen Cruikshank (safely down in Florida, probably authoring another of her fine bird books).

> . . . every year hath its winter,
> And every year hath its rain—
> But a day is always coming
> When the birds go north again.

A woman named Ella Higginson wrote that; I hope she is right.

It doesn't help my depression to open an anthology of school poems my daughter has sent me (Carleton Schreider, the *Brooks Anthology*), and read on the first page about a man living in the wilderness:

> Unseen within him broods a hardness
> A loneliness which has grown over the years.
> And now this man lives alone in the dark woods,
> To pass away the years.

Is this also me? Run from life, hiding on this mountain? A frightening thought.

Letter to Grandson Peter, at St. John's College, Santa Fe

"What was it that Japanese poet wrote? 'If we keep within our heart a green bough there will come, one day, a singing bird'? Something like that. I'm not handy to a library, you look it up. Onitsura, that was his name. Or do they teach you only Greek and astronomy?"

Obviously the Spring Solstice has me down.

March 22nd

To celebrate Spring I open another net in Sycamore Canyon, having seen a thrush and a towhee foraging in the leaves on the far side of its creekbed. This is also full of rocks, but if I can take a bird it will be worth picking my way across. So what do I take? A thrush and a towhee.

The stream edge opens out at this sheltered, sunny curve into a miniature flood plain, sandy, I needn't watch my every step. A hawk screams and flies off behind trees. Then suddenly, coasting down from the Peak at tree-top level, inspecting my labors, I see an eagle! Its head shines pure white. A BALD EAGLE! They are not supposed to be here! Am I getting at last a rare bird, an incredible record? I run into the open, the bird so low I don't need binoculars. As it passes over head the light shifts, that white shining head normalizes into the brown of the Golden before I have raced back to the Ranch and rushed to Tucson to report A Marvelous Discovery. . . . The experienced birder's motto is "Always Take a Second Look." Oh pshaw. (Every day I get more experienced.)

March 23rd

Two young men who went through this morning returned disappointed and weary. They had lost the washed-out trail, did not reach the Peak. We perch on the porch edge in the late sun, eating apples and chatting. With delight they comment on the silence. I agree.

"It's marvelous," I tell them. "Except for those damned flyboys. Almost every day they roar over from the Air Force base at Tucson; two, three, four, or five of them on their way to the bombing range at Ajo."

They scream into this peaceful bowl, shattering the quiet, sending my fingers to my ears. I hate them.

The men regard each other ruefully. They are flyboys!

"But we aren't the noisiest," they try to assuage me. "Haven't you noticed a difference in the planes?"

I haven't. They go too fast, I am too vexed. We all laugh. They are being transferred to England and don't want to go. This is their last day off.

I fetch the register and have them write their occupation after their names. I keep a record for The Conservancy of who comes here. Largely professional, their backgrounds are listed as accounting, architecture, biology, bird carving, botany, carpentry, conservation, engineering, geology, hydrology, medicine, painting, photography, physics. There have also been a clerk, a social worker, the Border Patrol, the Department of Public Safety, the religious retreat group. Students are the largest category. Even with hostile weather the score for the winter quarter has been 110, and now I am adding two Air Force pilots.

Note: A few days later Bill brought a Conservancy Field

Trip in. He listened patiently as usual to my complaints about the loneliness, the lack of occupation, of friends. At this point two planes roared over the Peak in formation. They flew low, dipped their wings, circled the Ranch twice, dipped again, and were off. Bill looked at me with amusement.

"You say you have no friends?" My flyboys, off to England!

March 25th

It really is Spring. Songs ring cheerily about, I band two Scott's orioles, named for the commander of the American forces in the Mexican war by one of his lieutenants. It had been described and named *parisorum* in 1837 by a brother of Napoleon, but the American name stuck. I also band a Wied's flycatcher. Its name came from a German prince who chased birds in Brazil and North America. How men got around in the nineteenth century!

"Are you sure it was a Wied's?" my mentors questioned me later, the record being early.

Indeed I am. These western flycatchers are rare in South Florida, but I took three there over the years, and had them corroborated. So as to be sure not to confuse them with the common (in Florida) Great Crested, I carry samples of the tail feathers of both, neatly labeled, in my banding box. Probably the only bander with such equipment. The Ash-throated here is similar. Its tail also has an identifying pattern. So, since the above questioning I have added a third envelope, with Ash-throated's feathers in it. Not the whole tail— I just thieved a little.

Occasionally I get queries from Humane Society types asking about how hurtful netting must be to birds, if damage to their eyes (nonsense!) from nets, the trauma of capture is worth any information we might obtain? If there isn't already enough known about birds? I could live a hundred years and not learn all I need to know about birds! My answer is that their money should go for green space, for safe habitat for birds to live in; that I see more birds dead on the road in a hundred miles, killed by man with no benefit to science, than might die from my handling in many years. Information derived from marking wild birds is of immense value to our understanding of their lives and needs to better protect them.

I give talks on birds in the hand. In an hour I can present only the most simplified information. It is astonishing, horrifying how much of this is new to the average citizen, how little he knows about other creatures in his world. TV is encouraging an interest—probably why I get asked to lecture. These same ignorant citizens must vote for preservation of marshes, creation of wilderness areas, decide in their communities what vegetation to save, what to plant around schools and churches and industrial plants and their homes, unaware, obviously, that their decisions affect wildlife.

At dusk a striped skunk escorts me across the Creek, a small handsome creature walking slowly. So do I. Its plumed tail waving in the beam of my flashlight makes me nervous. Skunk oil is reputed good for lame joints. If I rubbed some on my hip could I skip more nimbly over these boulders? A fishing guide once told me skunk meat was delicious, but the only man I know who would be willing and able to trap and dress skunks for me is Durward Allen, probably up on Isle Royale studying the wolves he has made famous. I will settle for canned corned beef.

Huzza! I climb the mountain! Well, its shoulder, I really can't boast.

The first reported conquest of that crevassed rectangular granite slab was by two men who made it to the Peak in 1897, stoked by sauerkraut and hot chilis. They had few followers until 1933, when the CCC constructed a trail. Since then innumerable men and some women have scaled it, including former Supreme Court Justice William O. Douglas. (There would be a name for the Register!) Baboquivari has a redoubtable reputation among climbers, whether or not people can pronounce it (the ascent is on the *qui*). My Christmas mail had several good wishes from men who had climbed it—or failed to—in their college days, and greatly envied me living in its shadow.

The more ambitious arrive with ropes and pitons and overnight packs and cheerful energy (and self-confidence) to attempt the east face with its 1,200-foot overhang. The Rescue Squad knows that overhang well. The less ambitious and day visitors hunt the trail that leads over the saddle into Papago country. This leads to a spring, I am told, a good campground, and eventually to the summit. There is a legend that someone wanted to erect a radio beacon up there once, but the surveyor, a city man, was trapped for three days by clouds and turned in a negative report.

I say "hunt" the trail because it is so badly washed out this year that many miss their way, returning dejected and sore-legged, happy to sit and chat. The more experienced insist it is easy. Three merry fellows who signed the register one recent morning, not too early, knocked at my door in black night to report they were safely down. How they had managed that treacherous creekbed in moonlight I couldn't believe. When I cross it at night I carry *two* flashlights, in case one conks out. No fourteen-hour romp up that forbidding, beautiful hunk of stone for me, not even the easy way. They hadn't heard any owls.

> There's something about a mountain that engraves itself upon a man's emotions. . . . Mountains are barriers. Mountains are adventure. . . . Who can stand in the presence of a mountain and remain unchanged?
>
> It was not altogether a matter of mysticism that prompted ancients to the belief that their gods dwelt in the high places of this earth. By whatever name we call them those gods still dwell there. (Hal Borland, *Our Natural World*)

I don't feel magnificent, as Borland suggests in a further sentence, when I look at Baboquivari. Incompetent is a better word. All winter I have been eyeing that skyline ridge running south from the base of its slab. I have figured that if I mount the first steep slope, by zigging and zagging always on the spines of the ridges I might be able to reach the horizon. The cows do, I see them with my telescope. I told Alice of this ambition. She went up and down in one afternoon, reporting that it was feasible, although mighty steep at the end. Alice is built like a deer, slim and long-legged, and twenty-nine. I am none of those things, and so far have avoided heaving myself up even that first hill.

Today is clear and blue. A north wind blows. Small birds wind-tightened in nets would be in trouble. I have acknowledged my last letter. I don't need to bake bread. I am full of energy, my gimpy hip is not troubling me and in another week those rattlesnakes may be out. I eat a big breakafast, chew two vitamins instead of one, weigh the advantage of a red beret for visibility against my straw sun hat, of a bright sweater against the torn dun one that would be the same color as the winter grass if a helicopter should come looking for me (you have to think of everything). I put a health cooky in my pocket, thermos and camera in my pack, binoculars as always around my neck, and am off. No sandwich or apple—I will be back for a late lunch. (Note: I didn't know how late.)

I climb and I climb. It's marvelous. I am right about the spines of the ridges. I move higher and higher on them, avoiding arroyos and canyons. The cows have made trails, and are clumped in the highest mesquite thicket, not eager to let me pass. Do range cattle charge people? Holding my sotol staff at the ready I talk soothingly and ease through them. Sotols are yuccas. At this time of year their dry stalks dot the slopes like exclamation points. How I should like to see them in bloom, instead of in their winter brown!

The scenic saguaros don't grow at Baboquivari, although there are many on the slopes and ridges around Tucson. Why? Altitude? Soil? Perhaps they are over on the other side, by Ajo. The Papagos have harvested the ruby-red fruits that circle their lofty tops it is said, since the days that Iitoi gave them life. They eat the sweet fruit raw; cook it into jam and syrup, make it into the traditional wine for their rain ceremonies. The men also traditionally paint the soles of their feet red with it, before ceremonies, so that when they pass out their feet are decorative! The women harvest buds from that awful cholla, too; prickly pear fruit, mesquite beans, and the yucca bananas. I meditate on their patience and endurance, dealing with all those thorns in baking heat, and think of the broccoli in my fridge that Alice has sent up. I, with my soft white-woman ways, am surely an interloper in Elder Brother's land. Mounting the next rise I thank him for *his* patience, and look for mesquite beans on the trees, but find none. It is the wrong season.

Now I am out of cow paths, wonderfully high. Far below the Ranch is tiny, with toy outbuildings and water tanks. I hadn't realized it spread so widely. My eyes follow the road where it curves out past the windmill, parallels the Creek, disappears, curls out far down the open valley. I see no dust rising, the Road Man is not at work. Various slopes I have climbed for photography during the winter look inconsequential. Even the crenelated Rhyolites and the tapering dyke of the Dragon's Tail cease to be imposing. I've wanted to climb there, but see I needn't. Another, higher range shuts off any view toward Kitt Peak and Tucson. There is virgin grassland somewhere up there, but my ignorance wouldn't recognize it.

Besides, all this climbing isn't easy. I long ago took off my sweater.

I scramble, pulling up with my staff. Rancher has ordered me to carry it. It acts as a third leg, he says correctly, and slows falls. It also uses an arm muscle I don't recognize.

A horse passed this way, long ago. Deer also have left sign but not trails, bounding over terrain I find more and more difficult. Not too far above me is the horizon's rim. The wide slopes have narrowed to rocky spines. I puff to the top of each one—surely the last? Each time above me is another hillock, a small climb, maybe only fifty feet up. Just one more, I can make it. Then another, damn it. At one point I look down and out over space, above a deep canyon, with sheer rock rising—the base of Baboquivari. I think of cheating, of taking photographs here and claiming, if ever I give a program on the Ranch, that this is the other side. But I haven't made it this far not to see what really I have come for—Mexico, California, maybe even a flyboy loosening his load of bombs. (Not real bombs, they assured me.) Hillock above hillock above hillock . . .

You are a fool to keep going, my sensible self scolds. You are tired. You will fall, and who will find you? Don't you notice that when you stop, lie down to rest, above you against the blue sky a raven flies over and eyes you with evil intent?

What better do I have to do? my cheery self counters. It is a gorgeous day, why can't I play hooky? Is it a plain old Common raven, or a White-necked one? They look alike.

The cat's claw has long since given out. Now in between the talus I am trying to dodge clumps of low cactus that looks like overgrown chives and is guaranteed to tattoo a leg or a backside. Lechuguilla (I think). The higher I go the thicker it grows until it is a veritable pasture, like grass. At lower elevations the javelina root it up to eat the onionlike bulbs, but no javelina has made it up here on stumpy legs. I skin under what must be the Ranch fence—aha, now I am in Papago territory. No one is in sight.

Airy depths open between me and their sacred Peak, now so close, so bright. What looks like varicolored algae on its rocks is probably vegetation and tall trees. On my other side depths are also airy, with White-throated swifts surfboarding in the wind against the cliffs. I surmount a final rise. I could go higher, but now at last I am on the rim, and see what I have come for—miles and miles and miles of blue space between me and Yuma, between me and Mexico, the great world mine. Ridges and peaks and canyons on every side, Baboquivari Peak across just one yawning gap. I move toward this cautiously, peer down a cliff face, and realize I am standing where I had aimed my camera an hour ago. If I had known this was what I had to reach I would have quit down there and gone home for lunch. Long ago I ate my cooky. I also abandoned my thermos and sweater somewhere below those hillocks, expecting to be back in ten minutes. I hope I find them! The Ranch went out of sight many ridges ago. There is hamburger down there, and a pan of brownies.

Descending uses different muscles. There is no way I can get lost. Terra firma drops off on either side of me, something I had not noticed as I climbed, looking always up. Or down, rather, at that lechuguilla. Solid outcrop gives way to broken rock with a few pinyon pines growing in it, and wind-warped shrubs: a small bird in one, he hid. As the outcrop becomes more broken the footing comes more chancy. I don't wear boots, they are heavy, clumsy. Besides, I bought mine on a hot afternoon when my feet were swollen, so they are too big.

Coming up I could test a rock before heaving myself onto

it. Going down the biggest can start slides, taking a climber with them. As they grow smaller they nip at my heels, rolling along behind me. I am aware, again, that if I fall or wrench or break there will be no one missing me for days. Or weeks. Not knowing where I have gone. This makes for slow progress, although I long ago forswore nervousness. You become a fatalist when you live alone.

I reach the cat's claw. I reach the mesquite. I reach the cows and the lookout where I had stopped to photograph the Ranch because I was so high. My muscles protest every step. I reach the shale and start sliding. I miss the cow path to the Creek and slide, on purpose this time, over its edge and onto its boulders. Blue jeans can take a lot of punishment.

No rattlesnakes. One leg is tatooed by lechuguilla. Only one cactus spine. That hamburger is delicious. If, of course, burned.

March 26th

Every day Spring. A Bullock's oriole has joined the peacocks in the tree over the chicken coops, and there is an influx of sparrows along the road. Don't ask me what kinds, see all my comments on sparrows in the bush. I don't get any in the hand, drat it, although I set an extra net where they were. Yesterday. Today they are gone, all I have to show for my chopping and clearing are scratches.

William Bullock was the proprietor of a museum in London. He collected birds in a mine near Mexico City. The oriole was named for him by Swainson, for whom Swainson's thrush is named, as are Swainson's hawk and Swainson's warbler. Audubon named these latter. Swainson also was an Englishman, a prominent naturalist and traveler who ended up as an attorney-general in New Zealand. (The English get around.)

I learn all this from Ernie Choate's book. How would I amuse myself evenings, without Ernie in my lamplight? Ernie disapproves of my life style. He cooked for me one week, in a remote fishing camp in the Everglades. I brought him in a red-shouldered hawk from a net in a mangrove swamp. I was muddy and slightly damaged: the hawk wasn't, just angry. Ernie wrote me at Christmas that I have a talent for living in uncomfortable places. He is right. I will tell him about burned toast and hash and peacocks, and hear his scornful grunt clear across the continent.

The Bullock's has been tossed into the pot recently as a subspecies with the Baltimore oriole, both now going under the colorless name of Northern oriole. The Baltimore won its name from the colors of the colonial proprietors of Maryland. Too bad to lose all that history. You might as well learn all about a bird you can while you are examining its plumage.

Now that the juncos have left (the Oregons are all gone, a few Gray-headed linger), Sycamore Canyon is my most productive area. The wide view down the valley is an hourly pleasure, as are the Crissal thrasher singing from a bare snag on my way, the Black-throated sparrow on his bush, an Acorn woodpecker with his comical black, white, and red clown face, the Ash-throated flycatcher on territory, and the jays talking. Here is where the first mariposa lilies bloomed, where the ground hugging belly flowers came out first, where there is a western milkweed, *Asclepias asperula,* with closed green flowers. Flowers are mighty rare on these hills, I treasure every one of them. Here is where the first mesquite leafed out, promising shade at last for nets. For a day or two on my runs over here I picked up rocks in the path so I could safely look around instead of down. The horses, full of spring zest, romped through and kicked them back, with interest, every evening: this ridge seems to be their favorite hangout.

Each time I mount the student steps, irregular but solid, built with strong young hands and gaiety, I thank them.

March 27th

The Road Man promised. He had several times before, but not
personally to me. He came up the other day with Rancher.
We had a beer and a sandwich on the bare springs of the swing
while he whittled a wedge to repair my axe. He was a friendly,
nice man, a hale seventy years. If he had been sick all winter,
as he reported, he didn't look it. Last night in Tucson I learned
that instead of starting our road, as he had promised, he has
taken an easier job at an adjoining ranch.

Rancher is distressed by his lack of probity, and also because
Rancher worries, with good weather, about my car being vandalized. The Nature Conservancy is distressed because if the
propane gives out and the truck can't—or won't—get in, I
will have to leave; and because I threaten that now the water
in the second ford is low enough for me to steer between boulders (perhaps), I am going to drive through and try to make it

up to the windmill, a mile nearer to pack supplies in. I am distressed because after sticking out the weather all winter I would hate to have to leave just as spring migration starts.

At the moment I am raging angry at not being able to drive the whole way to the Ranch. As I write this, I am huddled in my car at the thorn tree in driving rain, inadequately dressed. One way to shelter is two miles on foot, carrying groceries. The other is seventy miles, back to Tucson, where I started from at noon. The newspaper at Three Points, last outpost of civilization, milk, and bananas, headlined WET ALL DAY. The clouds are low. When they break I see sheets of rain curtaining the Peak.

Oh, well—you take life as it comes. I have bananas, some terrible store cookies, raw eggs, if they haven't scrambled en route, and more than two weeks' mail that I sat up last night sorting. (Insurance companies, credit card companies and tax offices make no allowance for where you live.) The back of my wagon is long enough to sleep in if the storm continues— between the shovel and the bags of groceries and the Patience plant I bought. Something around here has to be patient. And how am I to get that up mountain? Never mind, I will, flowers are my comfort.

I slept badly in Tucson last night. Not because of a tele phone call telling me that a nine-year-old vandal had smashed into my Cape Cod home, but because the Rocs' new, unhappy Siamese cat decided my friendly back rubbings, my room, and my bed were an assuagement for its loneliness in strange sur roundings. It was an uneasy night . . .

Pale yellow composites with silver foliage had rimmed the roadside on my rainy drive today. Along the cattle track inside the gate lupine was a low thick carpet of blue and green. Standing among these were purple columbine and tall, coarse purple thistles, and a variety of tiny crucifers frosted or spangled with rain.

I make it to the cabin finally. The rain slackens, continues on and off. A hundred steps, then a pause to puff and adjust the pack straps cutting my shoulders, to shift the insulated bag to the other hand. As always I am carrying too much, but I never know when—or if—someone will arrive to bring up what I have left in the car. It may be tomorrow, or two weeks from tomorrow, by which time I will have come down for the load myself. Rain waters the Patience plant in my free hand. The thermometer at my door reads 55 degrees. Nothing that a hot bath and a hot rum lemonade won't alleviate.

March 29th

Clearing but still cold. My oldest son arrives with his family, Bill, Bill's Aunt Elizabeth, and a picnic lunch. And more bananas. I'll bet I don't eat another banana for a year. The men and Aunt Elizabeth climb the hills. My daughter-in-law, recuperating from chicken pox at age fifty, stretches out in the deck chair between lettuce flats on the warm sunporch. My young grandchildren play cards—so much for a grandmother's genes! They are the space, TV, and computer generation. Mountains are not for them, although they give the peacocks an astonished glance.

March 31st

That familiar carol in the yard has to be a robin, and it is! Like cardinals, robins to me are an eastern dooryard bird. In Buffalo they were a joyful sound, declaring the long winter over. One, on his return each spring, flew to my feeding tray and squawked lustily for a welcome of stale bread. White; he wouldn't touch brown.

Alas, alas, in these dry hills the waves of colorful migrant warblers and other small birds we expected do not come through, the Ranch must be too high. The desert floor was thronged with sparrows the other day. What I am getting is flycatchers. If you will turn to page 198 in *Birds of North America: A Guide to Field Identification,* by Robbins, Bruun, Zim, and Singer (Golden Press, paperback $4.95, the glue doesn't hold up, get the hard cover), by far the best guide for identification, you will read:

> THE GENUS EMPIDONAX, the most difficult genus of North American flycatchers. Species are frequently impossible to identify in the field. All are small, short-tailed flycatchers with eye rings and wing bars. Wing bars of immature are more buffy than adult's. . . . Size differences are slight and overlapping. With experience most can be identified on the breeding ground when singing and when habitat provides a clue.

THE GENUS EMPIDONAX is what I am getting, six of the seven species recorded here. Since they are changing habitats and don't sing, I lack these clues. I check their coloration. I measure the length of this feather as compared to that, the depth of the fork (if any) in their tails, the bill length from the nostril, the extent of light and dark in their mandibles (upper and lower bills). None of them wholly fits the definitions in the scholarly papers I have to instruct me. The papers differ, too. I moan when I see still another of these nondescripts awaiting release. Also they are given to getting netted at dusk, so I must untangle them by flashlight and study them by lantern, which surely affects color decisions. The only one I feel I really know from my eastern work is not supposed to be here, but I have taken five today. Well, what have I been sent here for, except to get what no one expects? So on my sheet I write boldly, LEAST FLYCATCHER.

You learn early when you deal with birds never to make a positive statement. Time and again the birds or your betters will prove you wrong. Human nature being as it is, of course you keep right on making statements and having to eat crow. The quotation above you have read (I hope). Following is what Gale Monson, wishing not to hurt my feelings, wrote when he received my records.

> In Arizona it is a rare occasion to find a Least. . . . Any bird with tail measurements between 62 and 68 mm is suspect to misidentification in the hand—confusion with Hammond's mostly, but even possibly with some Duskys. So I generally say that identifying these birds, unless they are extreme in size, is risky and must be left to specimens of known sex being identified by an expert with long experience and good series of comparable specimens. You may have reached the same conclusion.

That is a friendly last sentence. You see why this hobby of mine is not all beer and skittles?

April Fools' Day

Off to Tumacacori to a meeting of the Santa Cruz Forum of the Greater Outdoors, a mouth-filling name. Rancher has supported me and my work all winter, fetched in those loads of mesquite and gallons of milk, the least I can do is support his conservation group. Besides, I'm bored. Both those names (I can't pronounce Tumacacori) promise something different from life up here. There is to be a field trip—take work clothes; a banquet—take dress clothes. Why do groups term their dinners banquets?

I allow plenty of time. Nothing to do here anyway. I make a sandwich, fill the thermos (always take food). Reaching the highway I cross the desert to the crossroads town—if you can call its few buildings that—of Arivaca. Two traffic signs on the empty miles inform me that this is an UNPAVED ROAD— one as I turn onto it, another several miles in. As if among the dust and ruts a driver would not have noticed! Warning signs are still up and a little water runs in a dip that in December shut residents off for weeks.

On the far side of Altar Valley I drive through more mountains, emerging on the broad highway to Nogales. It runs south through the hundred-mile Santa Cruz Basin. In 1864 grass grew two and a half feet high in this valley, bending to the wind, cloud-shadowed like a sea. Now this verdance is only hinted at in the desert oasis of a sewage treatment plant.

Underneath the Basin lies—lay—a treasure of water now being withdrawn faster than nature can replace it. The hills are laced with roads waiting for development that will use more.

Our Forum is to meet at the Tumacacori Mission just down the road from Tubac. De Anza marshaled his great trek across the desert to California there, passing through Borrego Springs and the Park that now commemorates him. Did he travel in snow, I wonder? Did he have to cross those many Dips as I did in torrential downpours?

The Spanish settlement was later an important U.S. military post in the Indian wars. Its former glory is shrunk to a circular hamlet of small craft shops with adobe walls, and flowers glowing in Mexican pots by their doors. Arty, but relatively honest in its art. A dusty park with benches under a few trees provides rest for those who come to view the dusty fort. The custodian does not seem surprised at my reluctance to pay fifty cents to view his few bare rooms. What I am looking for is not history, but a shop somewhere in that circle called The Potted Owl, where I hope to find Maxine Guy, co-author of *Care of the Feathered and Furred,* a bible for anyone raising infant or injured birds, or small mammals. I take in infant or injured birds only when forced to, but I have been grateful for her advice many a time and am curious to see how she lives, what she may have in cartons in her kitchen, or in her aviaries. She is a friend of someone whose name I can't remember, I promised to look her up.

I do. She turns out to be a friendly, handsome woman, eating her sandwich (I just politely swallowed mine outside) behind an informal sales room with mugs, plates, and a potter's wheel. She makes no fuss about being interrupted, but goes on eating, which is how I like it. She sits on her side of a counter, in the kitchen. I sit on the other, in the living room.

Around and around us, beside and behind, in tireless play frolic a young bobcat and an equal-sized house cat, springing out at each other from couches and chairs, ambushing, leaping. Marvelous!

She shows me the owls caged at her back door. Everyone who takes in birds to mend has one owl—or six. They are long-lived. Zoos and museums already have one—or six—and don't want another. Great Horned owls, which is what they usually are, make poor household pets, so us avian Florence Nightingales are stuck with them. We discuss owl diets and exercise (we should both have more interest in our own) and I leave; wanting to stay longer but wishing to be mannerly.

I still have a half hour to spend. At the end of the road well-dressed people are going into an art gallery. I haven't seen well-dressed people or an art gallery for some time, not being able to get to the galleries and museums of Tucson, as I had hoped. So I follow and find myself at an Opening, with punch and a table of delicious-looking tidbits. An uninvited interloper, conscious of my attire, I decide that if I resolutely ignore the free food table it should be all right for me to wander about in my jeans. Artists like to have their work admired. I spend the half hour very pleasantly, enjoying the clothes and chatting people as much as the portraits. No one gives me a dirty look. I refuse an offer of punch and leave with my honor unsmirched.

The Forum, I had thought, was to be a group of ranchers, and maybe this assemblage is. They appear, however, more to be well turned out retirees to the Sun Belt, in spanking clean stripes and plaids, ties, straw hats (the men); sports clothes of various elegance (the ladies). Not what I expect of desert ranchers. I see a woman I had met in Tucson at a cocktail party and had had considerable conversation with. Her eyes slide over me with no recognition. I arrange to walk along the road with her for a bit. Still no recognition. That's the way I feel about cocktail parties: chatter, chatter, chatter to people you will rarely see—or recognize—again. That's the way I feel about me in a group of people—a ghost, not even seen. Maybe if I liked martinis I would do better?

The hotel we go to, still under construction, has so little character it could be in California, Hilton Head, the Caribbean, or Virginia—although Nogales and Mexico are only a few miles down the highway. Inside its one western touch is a raised center fireplace. Outside its hill commands a stunning panorama of the Santa Cruz valley, circled many miles distant by mountain ranges. Across the river a new town is rising. Everywhere the hills are ribboned with roads that some day, developers evidently hope, will be edged with homes. Where will the water come from? Rio Rico translates as Rich River, and so its flood plain was. Today the Santa Cruz is a shallow stream. We are taken on a field trip to see some of the damage done when it rampaged in mid-December, ripping out bridges, trees—a two hundred-year-old cottonwood lies in the gravel, ugly, before us. Swimming pools were torn out, agricultural fields gutted. The people who had built fine homes across the river now must drive fifteen and twenty miles south and around through Nogales to reach them.

We are shown the foundations of the last bridge, and bridges before that. We drive on a ravaged road that used to border the river, now bordered by piles of discarded cars and other heavy hardware brought in in a desperate effort to control the current. At dinner there is much discussion of what can be done to prevent such destruction again; of what sorts of trees, forbs (these are shrubs, I think), and grasses could be planted to hold the banks. A man from the Army Corps of Engineers stands up. He is working on how bridges and homes in Tucson can be protected from recurrent flooding.

"I am sorry to tell you there is nothing you can do, unless you line the river channel for its total length with cement—an improbable and economically impossible project."

An amazing statement coming from the Corps, but he is young, a new generation. He sobers his audience. They are learning the lesson anyone living on a flood plain must learn. Rivers give rich soil, fine crops, and beauty. But sooner or later, in a hundred years, tomorrow, they take these away: and you too, if you are so ill-advised as to build beside them.

I hunt up Maxine and greatly enjoy my evening.

Next day I play hooky. Instead of rushing home to those empty nets I poke through Indian missions and historical monuments, explore side roads, forget the long way I must retrace. I drive over the river, up and down the hills of the new town. Except for its view over limitless space it could be a new suburb anywhere: the houses close together, householders watering their new shrubs (forbs?), picking up children's toys. I drive around a complex of sewage ponds well known to birders, admiring the ducks that find a refuge, and, I suppose, sustenance there. Rainbows rise from spraying sheets of water, small birds are in the trees. It is civilized, orderly, refreshing. I need Joe Lund, who first brought me here. He can identify any duck by a flick of its wing, and a hawk at any distance.

This broad valley has many hawks. I keep stopping—illegally, I learn from a police officer—on the dangerous high-speed highway to study them with binoculars, to try to figure them out from my bird guide. Hawks go through several plumages before they reach full adult feathering, I class them with sparrows and peeps (small sandpipers) as being difficult to call accurately. For me, anyway; lots of my friends can, giving me an inferiority complex. It is fun to try to call them, though, when no one is around to make you sensitive to your ignorance. Until the police interrupt your fun.

I can't even see Baboquivari's thumb rising against the sky until I am within thirty miles, and realize that if I am to be home before dark I had better hurry.

April 4th. Letter to Ann and Harvey Gaylord

"My mail is always full of wonderful things. Like applications for color-banding Least Tern, three-pound reports from the New Jersey Dept. of Endangered Species, requests from people wanting to know about all the exotic species I must be taking. When I get the mail . . .

"Spring is here. The Road Man's tractor-bulldozer is a mile down canyon. Broken. It smells. His idea of a passable road and mine are not the same, but if I bully him he may quit entirely. I have already tried pleading, diplomacy, and other gambits.

"Your friend Bix is reputed to be coming to call on me. Company!

"I've a Hooded oriole at my syrup feeder, a squirrel on the seed feeder, a Bewick's wren at peanut butter, and peacocks perched outside my windows wanting to know what am I doing inside, and why didn't I put out more food (for the towhees and juncos) for them to enjoy?

"Because it is blowing like crazy the only nets I have open are in another canyon, in a sheltered groove. Once I clamber across the creekbed it is a pretty walk over there on a horse trail through mesquite slopes. A fine way to avoid housework.

"I trust you are both in health and rolling the croquet field. I trust you notice this machine is spelling better."

April 5th

What pleases me about overnight visitors—I have another—
aside from my delight in their company and my appreciation
of the effort they have made to get here is their connotation of
the word "early."

Vim Wright comes from rainy Seattle. She arrived unex-
pectedly with Bill, a sackful of fruit juices, tortillas, sherry,
and other delicacies, with news of the outside world and cities.
She serves on a Presidential Commission on shale oil. Her brain
awes me, but mercifully she keeps it under wraps. Past bedtime we take her sleeping bag and flashlight over to the Big
House. I retrieve the key to upstairs from a spot the peacocks
have not yet found and usher her into the dormitories. She is
insistent upon using the one early sunlight will flood.

"It will be early," I warn her—she is a night person. But
never mind, the peacocks will have woken her before then
anyway. It is breeding season and their raucous cries resound
with daily increasing decibels.

She is delighted. The prospect of peacocks honking, sun
pouring into her room no matter how early, is Vacation. At
nine the next morning she saunters into the cabin. My nets

have been open for two hours—I am a morning person. But my joy at having a visitor does not depend on hours.

Whether personal friends, or hikers, or just the curious who have heard of the Ranch and come to see it, visitors are easily separated. There are those who glow with enthusiasm; others whose gaze fastens on the old chicken coops and trash barrels, the sagging shed doors. They don't notice a Canyon wren slipping under one of the latter, taking feathers to its nest, or the phoebe on her rafter. Invariably they suggest I should have a dog for protection. Well, in four months I have not been attacked by anything but mice and cat's claw. I should carry dog food in two miles? I have trouble enough getting tuna fish here. What I need are computerized sneakers that will tell me whether the next rock I step on will be firm or twist under my foot, but I don't want to alarm them with this remark. No electricity? They marvel. No telephone?

If they arrived in a vehicle its unpleasant odor lingers after they have left, the air slow to cleanse its weight, as it is to diffuse their cigarette smoke. They accept instant coffee, but I can tell who has an electric percolator plugged in at home, using up energy.

None of this nonsense from Vim! She is a political animal, high in her field. Currently teaching grad students, she says with a happy grin, how to infiltrate the new conservation ethics into their fields of law and public relations. We climb ridges and photograph each other standing against space. Back, we settle down with mugs of tea and watch a hummingbird pull strands from an old electric wire. It shapes this manna with its breast into a nest in the vine on my cabin—Vim's bright-eyed discovery. We try to determine with our binoculars whether or not it has on its throat the small speckles that identify the Broad-bill. (It had, I saw them clearly the next day, but the bird left when Vim did, I never saw it again. No, she didn't steal it, she wrote me.) We sit, silent and companionable in the sun, eat the good food she has brought, and go to bed early. Next morning I regretfully walk her down to her car, hoping my mountain has refreshed her as much as she has refreshed me.

Shortly afterward a rancher rode in on a high horse, both literally and figuratively. Mad as a hornet. He was a big, handsome man, not about to give an inch, not about to believe what I told him.

Access to the Conservancy property runs across the neighboring ranch—a courtesy I was quickly given to understand that was not to be abused by the slighted deviation, by any vehicle. One of his men had seen a red sports car driving hell for leather where it shouldn't, and had traced its tracks to the windmill ford (where they would have disappeared in the Creek water, in either direction). My visitor made it clear that if I or The Conservancy could not control our friends I should pack my bags and leave, as the cattle gates would be padlocked. He had me so shaken that I couldn't remember for a moment that Vim's rented car had been left below Ford 2 and she had come in the rest of the way with Bill, whose Wagoneer is a bright yellow.

Once or twice on weekends I have heard a truck grind up to our parking lot with carousing young people in it, but when they have seen a hiker's vehicle or my signs of activity they have turned swiftly and skedaddled. Except for Bill and Vim there has been no one come to the Ranch at all in the past few days.

It took me a bit to calm him but eventually he was mellowed by my obvious bewilderment (he may not have known it was at the roughness of his manner). To a degree. He cast a measuring eye on Bill's tire tracks. Wider, he agreed, than those of a sports car, and was I *sure* Bill's car is yellow? He asked how long I would be staying, what was I doing here? That question! Even in jeans and my torn sweater I don't seem to fit the terrain, my presence is obviously a surprise to every visitor. On some days it is to me, too.

April 6th

I am getting a few migrants, all flycatchers. Measure, measure, measure. Monday I go Outside to get sneakers, see a friend in hospital, attend a meeting of the Tucson Audubon Society, and have tea with friends from our government days. I am told the Road Man has appreciably improved my passage, but only on the distant side of my car. I don't dare look at the gauge on the propane tank.

Rancher Brother and his son have come to count the cattle, which have dropped calves, I hear them bawling. I hold a male Hooded Oriole in fresh black and orange plumage to their ears so they can hear its swift heartbeat. Like a kitten purring. The fourteen-year-old embarrasses me by asking, "How many chambers are there in a bird's heart?"

I give him Sewall Pettingill's heavy textbook to search out this information for himself, which pleases him and lets me off the hook. He reports shortly, "Four chambers, just as in man." Later I see him studying the book by lamplight in the Big House.

In past years I have talked about birds and wildlife to innumerable schoolchildren who live on city streets or in the drab ends of towns; or in suburban, television, Little League habitats, never getting out into the woods. Many of them are starved for what I represent; they are stimulating audiences. Unfortunately, more are not.

"Why shouldn't I kill a frog? Bring home a turtle? What good is a tern? My mother *told* me to kill snakes."

But some who care go on to wildlife, forestry, ecology courses. Eventually, with instruction from teachers like Vim, they may teach their towns and industries and government agencies that if we do not save the diversity and natural resources of our planet (they won't mean just shale oil and coal and channeled rivers) mankind will be as endangered as the hundreds of plant and animal species we have wiped out in our last few technological, chemical decades.

At noon the next day Rancher Brother and his son hang up their saddles, rub down their horses and kitchen table, and leave, courteously taking in their truck some heavy parcels to store in town against my departure next month. Before they go the lad brings over two books on teen-age electronics and shows me astonishing gadgets a boy his age can make—his hobby. He is requiting me for the thrum of the oriole's heartbeat against his ear—my hobby. Like my young grandchildren he lives in a world I do not understand. I played with jackstraws, not electronics.

April 7th. Morning

I find a poor-will in my net at dawn. The Hopi Indians named the species Holchko, the Sleeper. Once thought to be only a folk tale, in 1946 Dr. E. C. Jaeger found a poor-will torpid in a cave in southern California and proved that the bird actually does hibernate. The bird returned to the same spot for four winters, and remained inactive for up to eighty-eight days. Its body temperature dropped to 30 percent below normal. What a lot we don't know about our cohabitors! The species has been proved to hibernate in the Tucson area also. They emerge, or come north from wherever, and start singing in March. After this cold winter my bird was smart to wait a few weeks. I have been hearing its thin, repetitive call. With dusk it falls silent, unlike its cousins the whip-poor-wills and chuck-will's-widows, which for hours never pause, and drive people crazy. I had a chuck in Florida whose evening song perch was ten feet from my bed. No wonder people throw shoes at them! Nice to hear from a distance, though.

John Burroughs once counted consecutive whip calls from his cabin on the Hudson River. My memory is that his score ran over eleven hundred before the bird quit. I should keep a file of these tidbits. However would I carry it around? I know for a fact that if you have eleven Barn swallow nests in your boathouse, and there are fourteen hours of daylight, as in the Adirondacks in early July, and if ornithologists are correct in stating that a swallow feeds its young every sixty seconds, your black fly and mosquito population will be reduced by 9,240 bristling mouthfuls a day. Jim Marble kept his boat in the boathouse I lived above, and wanted to tear out the nests. Young birds keep their nests clean by backing up to the edge and letting fly. This is sanitary for them, less so for your boathouse or porch (or you, if you are studying a hawk's nest). My statistics defeated Jim. If you are fussy, I told him, you can put a board, or hang a diaper of cloth or plastic under the nests. It will be only for a few weeks and is worth it. Easier than cleaning up after a dog. He settled for tearing out old electric wires the birds were using for perches. They moved to the windshield of his boat . . .

The Canyon wren is still carrying feathers under the door of the Cowboy Shack, emerging from a knothole on the far side. Phyrrhuloxia are incubating in a thicket nearby and come often to the feeder for extra energy. A Hooded oriole flies in for sugar syrup from a mustard jar. If the fox leaves any.

Noon:

This is the weather I have waited for these many weeks. I sit outside with a book, alternately hot or cool as puffy white clouds pass over the Peak. I am reading Stephen Levine's account of his year at another Conservancy sanctuary, not far from here, in the grasslands. Our experiences differ, but our philosophies are much the same. He writes with the eye and the felicity of phrase of a poet. *Planet Steward,* he titled it.

As my watch commands I set the book aside and stroll around the nets, savoring the silence, the south wind. There is no hurry; there will be no birds awaiting me. After a while in this work you develop ESP. I can even tell sometimes which net holds a bird, and go there first. Heavy ones like jays and dove and woodpeckers bounce and struggle and often kick free as I approach. Smaller ones lie quietly. Today there have been none since the poor-will. I should complain?

On the trail to Sycamore Canyon a road runner bounds like a miniature deer. A real deer watches me from a distance. A cottontailed rabbit with orange hind legs and orange fur down its nape hops out from under a bush, eyes me nervously, and leaves. A sparrow on a mesquite studies me without concern, secure in the power of its wings. Bird songs reminiscent but unrecognized arise from the next hill. A hummingbird with purple sideburns feeds at a tall thistle of the same color where no bloom had been open this morning. A miniature blue lily decorates a rock, standing sturdy in its three inches. Butter-flies accompany me, pausing, fluttering, disappearing as their wings fold. I sit on a rock and listen to the Creek. It is shrun-ken from the winter's brawlings, nearly dry. Down Canyon the valley opens out to the wide desert, a breathtaking view seen from this trail only. The distant ranges on the far side are like cardboard cutouts. I look daily down there as I pass, to see if dust is rising from the Road Man's machines, but have seen none.

It is Palm Sunday. Buds are pushing out on the mesquite, the last frost is past. This is the Indian legend—mesquite leafs only when there will be no more frost, as sure a sign of the resurgence of life in these bare foothills as are the trills of *Hyla crucifer* along my New England lane.

Mesquite. All winter it has torn my clothing, my arms, my face. Its branches intrude on all my paths. Its tough wood has kept me warm. Its bare tracery has been lovely to look at. Eulalia Bourne, an extraordinary woman who once taught Mexicans in a ranch school across the Sasabe highway from our entrance, wrote this about mesquite, in *Woman in Levi's:*

> Its leaves are intricately graceful. In springtime, the loveliest color in rangeland is that of its tender new green. Its yellow blossoms, protected by business-like thorns, are fragrant feasts for bees and butterflies and other insect life. Its roots will reach astonishing depths to pick up precious water, or on rock-based land run laterally for twenty to forty or more feet to gather moisture and store it up against a rainy day.

Mesquite trunks and branches make good fence posts and good firewood. They were used as beams by the cliff dwellers, and some still exist to be studied by anthropologists and archaeologists. The early padres and their native converts used mesquite wood in their missions: some . . . have endured for close to two centuries. Mesquite gum was used by the Indians to make dye and cement for their pottery. The bark has been used for medicine. As for its beans, dried, it would be hard to name anything in cattle country more nourishing to animals. The U.S. Cavalry bought them by the pound for their horses. The Indians that knew of them, ate them. Even dogs eat them.

Letter to Anne Rose. 7:00 A.M., *April 8th*

"A series of calm blue days. Shirtsleeve weather, delicious but unproductive. Earlier in the week after a hard north wind that stacked up migrants I took twenty birds in one day—my record. At Manomet Bird Observatory on Massachusetts Bay twenty birds an hour is nothing! Mostly flycatchers, which are a challenge to key out. The differences are subtle ones in the sizes and shapes of feathers, the amount of dusky in the tail. But today I make my rounds and come back empty-handed.

"The Peak is glowing orange and yellow and green; gold light floods down the slopes, bird songs I don't know flood from up the canyon. The wide white faces of the evening primrose (*Oenothera trichocalyx* to you, dear botanist; here it blooms only in the morning) are open where all winter a sheet of water has overflowed from the big water tank. Now that the creeks are nearly dry the deer come here to drink, at dawn and dusk. Fragrant lavender verbena (*laciniata?*— growing wild at 5,000 feet?) spreads its own sheet.

"In the early morning animal scents come clearly to my nostrils—from the horses, grazing nearby; from a skunk that walks my paths at night; from cattle across the fence. Whiffs from animals I can't place. Catkins on the Emory Oaks are golden; a few tentative buds of mesquite at last poke out green fingers. On the tips of their twigs, sleeping until sun warms them, I find butterflies that flit busily along the trails at noon. I may have to start studying butterflies, there are so many here; more than birds. Mostly tiny and too restless to identify. There is a black one as big as a hummingbird.

"I have been out early because now it is warm enough to enjoy going out, at night I leave nets open (at the top where a predator cannot reach) in the hope an owl or a poor-will may be snared. I check after supper, again at bedtime. The next canyon would be the best place for owls, but crossing the jumbled boulders of the creekbed—two creekbeds—is hazardous enough for my creaking limbs in the daytime. A flashlight lights almost nothing, so I now confine myself to the washes on this side where paths are mostly broad, open, and familiar to my sneakers. Last night was half moon. I climbed the nearest slope—steep!—on a cattle trail, listening for night birds. Nothing. I feel guilty. I should do this every night.

"Nets open, twigs and leaves removed, pole strings tightened, I return to the cabin with its own heavy scent and make my bed while the sausage cooks, water boils for coffee, and the homemade bread I am toasting in a heavy iron skillet burns. I attribute my rude health you so affectionately inquire for in part to charcoal. You and Vic eat it on your steaks, why not try it on breakfast muffins?"

Evening:
I have read that starlight falls to earth in measurable, if min-

uscule quantities—one ten-thousandth of an ounce to a square mile a minute. Is it absorbed, I wondered as I climbed last night, by the earth like sunlight? Does it accumulate like snow, so that this glimmer on the hill I climb, that sheen on the Rhyolite Cliffs, is a dusting of starlight on the world? How many questions fill my days and nights, each time I step outside the door! The natural world did not impinge upon the classrooms of the girls' school I attended. I was exposed to reading and arithmetic and not enough history instead of learning the answers I now need. And when young Harvard men took me canoeing on the quiet reaches of the Charles River at night, education in the creatures and sounds and stirrings in the trees was not what they had in mind.

April 9th. Going Outside

I am late leaving, as usual. When at night I gather up paper-work, lists, bills, clothing, I forget that in the morning I must wash dishes, make the bed, feed the peacocks, water the garden in my greenhouse, carry in those plants of Rancher's Wife's that I had set out to get sun so they will be safe from our marauding avian beauties; pour sugar syrup for humming-birds, bait the mousetraps, make sandwiches for two days. (It saves time to eat lunch as I drive, and embarrassment if I arrive at Alice's at mealtime, which I always seem to.) The Hiker's Register, weighted with a rock, is out in the hope someone may see it.

I am off, carrying a light load of overnight needs, the brief-case, and cookies I made for the children. The day is blue and warm—no need for a sweater or raincoat (and wasn't I sorry when the temperature dropped below 50 degrees with rain and wind the next day!). I sling the half-empty pack on my back, anchor my straw hat over my ears, pick up the red insulated bag I'll bring frozen orange juice and chicken back in, and am off. With so little to carry I practically trot down the hills.

My car is there, muddy, dusty, but now on *this* side of Ford 2. It wasn't easy, but last time out I drove it there. (Not far.) It is scratched but faithful. Parked beside it, off the road, is a van with a wheel missing—climbers with a serious problem. Wonder how they got back to town?

I unlock, start the engine, buckle my safety belt, and shut the door. It doesn't shut. No matter what I try. Stubbornly determined to get my transportation closer to the Ranch, did the door resent jolting over that last outcrop of rock? Or has someone monkeyed with the lock? I contemplate the wheelless van . . .

Unless I hold the door it hangs loose, banging, swinging wide. I sacrifice the belt from my going-to-town suit, but it proves too soft. *Siempre hay una mosca en la sopa.* I lurch and twist the eight miles to the highway, steering with one hand, holding the door with the other. When one arm aches I shift to the other. Life is a challenge, I tell myself.

Thirty-five miles north, I stop at Three Points General Store to buy rope. And bananas for potassium—I need *something* to strengthen me. The storekeeper kindly shows me a trick that will close the door for the moment. A VW station in town shows me a better trick, and informs me the lock is broken. They don't have another in stock. Vibration, suggests the man cautiously, *might* have caused my problem. Or the driver of that van, anxious to go for repair?

Lunch with Alice and Henry on their terrace. I get my hair cut, go out for tea, go out for dinner, get lost in the maze of the University, arrive late at a meeting. There are people I want to see and people who want to see me, so I am last one out. I get lost again returning to the Roes', run my winter's slides through Alice's projector to see if any are good enough for a program, fall dreamlessly (and catlessly) to sleep.

April 10th

At 9 A.M. it is raining hard, and blowing. I *know* what the weather will be on Baboquivari. Sixty miles south it might be better, so I gamble and drive to Canelo Hills, also a Nature Conservancy Preserve. This is a sentimental journey. To pay a part of my debt to his friendship, I once bought an acre of that preserve as a memorial to Matt Baird. I want to see its famous cienaga, with rows of the old cottonwoods now so rare along Arizona streams. The streams are mighty rare, too. Cottonwoods suck up water, so ranchers and city fathers cut them down, heedless of the erosion they prevent, their welcome shade. Canelo has an old adobe building, and an everflowing stream. The National Audubon Society has taken possession of an adjoining property, which doubles the ecological value of this wet green belt.

Arizona is full of contrasts. Fifty miles south of Tucson hills are low and rolling, fields of grassland shimmer for silver miles. For directions I stop at a Forest Service sign where purple lilacs by the gate are as luxuriant as any in New England. A pleasant young woman accustomed to my question points the way. A pleasant young man, the manager at Canelo, greets me. But rain is scudding, the wind is bitter, his mother-in-law has just arrived, a baby cries. It is not the day to ask to be shown around, however much our positions as Residents give us in common.

In Patagonia I hunt up the homes of friends I have wanted to see all winter, leave disappointed notes and a cookie at their locked doors. (One pair was at Baboquivari, hunting me.) The road back, cross country, winds through a one-lane canyon pass. Fortunately I meet no one. Snow coats the slopes rising on either side. I stop at that excellent shopping mall in Green Valley for sneakers, having left my hiking shoes, like a dolt, in Tucson. The market is full of temptations. I ignore Easter lilies, much as I want one, but recklessly buy frozen raspberries and butter beans and okra and milk. The holiday is coming, I will celebrate.

Cross country again, again on an empty road. I wonder if I could change a tire? I never have needed to. Every other curve has a Dip warning sign. Far in the distance, against a gray but now rainless sky, Baboquivari rises, the highest point in this part of Arizona.

Whoops! The road in from the highway is decorated with lug marks! Problem areas have been assuaged, gullies filled. Rocks I have never met before have been knocked into the tracks. I am excited, I can make good time. The Road Man! His tractor is parked in my new slot. The tire-less van has vanished. I ease into its space against a boulder, sort purchases into pack and sacks and stride off, anxious to reach the windmill ford while I can still see my stepping stones.

The tractor worked hard. It breathed oil, and leaked it. And only a few hundred feet further up the road, past a fissured ridge my car could in no way surmount, it has laid a clear if humpy road I *could* have managed, all the way to Horse Bars Creek!

Never mind, Fisk, you have been sitting all day. Don't complain. The moon shines thinly behind clouds, the wind that gusts in my face and makes me shiver in my light clothing is soon blocked off by the rising hills. At the Ranch gate the horses come snuffling to see if I have Easter apples. A poorwill flutters from a mesquite, circles me as if in curiosity, and disappears into the dusk. Again I raise my eyes to the Peak, high, square, cold, and thank the gods that dwell there. Again they have brought me safely home, to toast and soup and a smidgen of rum in my tea, with a sackful of mail from those I love, from a busy world I do not need to live in.

April 11th

For the second time Helen and Joe Taylor appear at the horse
bars, hiking in from far down the road. What a gift of friendship! They have been camping at Organ Pipe Cactus Monu-
ment and are on their way back to Patagonia. I tell them about
the cooky at their door, and the nose smudges on windows of
their new house. I show them the Canyon wren's nest that now
has two eggs; they show me a Costa's hummingbird (named
for another Frenchman, a hummingbird-collector marquis.) We
listen to a Scott's oriole sing, and an Ash-throated flycatcher.
Joe holds the record for seeing more birds in the United States
than anyone. The Syracuse, N.Y. paper once ran a Sunday
supplement on his travels and birds, entitled "The Babe Ruth
of Birding," his rosy face wreathed in an Eskimo parka on its
full-page cover. So my treasures must be small to him, but he
does not let on. The three of us are friends from our years on
the Board of the Cornell Laboratory of Ornithology, a hard
place to get to in the blizzards of February. I often didn't make
it, but Joe always did. For twelve years. I respect him for more
than his bird list.

Good Friday, April 12th

Out by six, organizing my nets. There was wind in the night, they are caught on mesquite buds. BUDS, not twigs! After four months, BUDS! I am grateful. An oriole sings matins. I catch a three-gram female hummingbird that can be one of three species. Where is Joe, to tell me? Check its throat for speckles or red feather tips, its flank color, the pattern of its tail tip. Then I take a small olive flycatcher, which can be anything—measure, measure, measure. No matter what I decide and put on the form I have worked out, the men will tell me I am wrong. I've had a dozen of these in the last few days, coming north from their winter quarters in Mexico and South America. I wish they would stay there! They are fattening on insect hatches under the budding sycamore trees.

Around the nets again before breakfast. Sausage is browning, coffee made, an egg cracked, bread toasting in the skillet. I eat a big breakfast; no telling when lunch will be. But before I can pick up my fork I see a jeep drive around the bend and two young men debark, climbing gear over their shoulders. I turn off everything and go out with the Register. They left the city at 4:30 A.M. and are eager to be off.

Behind them, hiking, comes my visitor for the day, Sandy Hill, an English mining engineer from Brazil; a lean, pleasant fellow who has "ringed," as they term it in England, and wants to work with me. He has breakfasted only on doughnuts. I reactivate the skillets. Two more vehicles steam up, and eleven members of the Sierra Club of Los Angeles, Hiking Division, climb out. They camped down at the highway and are in a bustling hurry. Their agenda has three mountain summits to attain over the holiday. It is Easter weekend. I had forgotten. Not known.

Everybody takes off but Sandy, it takes a while. We eat finally. I show him about. The Canyon wren has four eggs, but the female is not yet incubating, there is another to come. He admires the Broad-billed hummer's nest on the cabin vine, no bigger than a quarter, and we grieve that it became deserted. The Say's phoebe hovers impatiently near the Big House porch with a feather in her bill, relining last year's nest. She obviously resents all this company. We go around the nets and compare English methods with American. The English are stricter and more solicitous in their handling of birds, so I am on my mettle. Sandy takes a broom handle for a staff and starts up the switchback ridges toward the skyline.

I now have five nets in Sycamore Canyon. Going to them is one of my real pleasures. It is easy walking, the view on the way is stupendous, there are always birds along it, and its different habitat has yielded new species for the list. On warm days cool air flows like a brook down the shaded creek. For cool days I have hollowed out a sunny seat against a rock where I can watch small birds go about their business, usually behind the opening leaves where they are hard to identify. For the last two days, though, I have taken nothing here.

Now I discover why. An irritated kek-kek-kek greets my arrival and a hawk moves from tree to tree. Behind the leaves, of course. I sit instantly. I heard this call two weeks ago. I saw the bird briefly another day. Now that I am motionless, look like a stump in my neutral clothing, it remains, working its way through an oak. It breaks off twigs and gathers them in its bill. I get a good look at the tail, then the breast, then finally the blue-crowned, unpatterned head. A Cooper's hawk!

This explains the old nest over my head that Herman was sure was an eagle's. A Cooper is an accipiter, one of the few hawks that feed mostly on small birds and mammals. DO NOT SHOOT THEM! 1) It is illegal. 2) They are a useful factor in the balance of nature. 3) A study done by a man named Meng (in New York State) showed that starlings are their most frequent catch, and one thing we don't need are starlings—a scourge to our native birds, farmers, and urban buildings.

Starlings are a European bird appropriately named *Sturnus vulgaris*. At least *I* consider *vulgaris* appropriate, watching their arrogant strut about lawns, their monopolizing of feeders. They gather in huge, noisy, filthy roosts in winter. We taxpayers must foot the bill for attempts to destroy them. They have spread uncontrolled since 1890 when sixty of them were liberated in Central Park and promptly started breeding under the eaves of The American Museum of Natural History. By 1952 they ranged across the United States and southern Canada, although they had not yet reached South Florida. In 1965, when I was moving into an apartment in downtown Homestead, twenty miles south of Miami, I saw a pair sneaking in and out of a tool shed across the street. Fresh from the District of Columbia, where they roost at night on government buildings by the hundred thousand, each one returning from its day in the country to a personal, individual perch, it didn't occur to me to report my sighting. I should have. December 3, 1965. Later I learned that this was the first observation this far south. I should have sneaked into that tool shed myself, too, and wrung their necks. By the next year the two had exploded to twenty, soon to sixty. When I left the area in 1978 there were hundreds, wheeling in formation over the town, interfering with the native birds.

They are handsome creatures in their way—glossy black,

speckled gold in winter, short-tailed. They swirl in flocks over the autumn fields, shifting direction as precisely, in loops and twists, as sandpipers. They were the most intelligent of any of the species I housed in the aviary I built when I moved outside town. Immediately they located food sources and secure hiding holes, immediately prying with sharp bills for possible escape holes under the wiring. I expect they sensed my destructive thoughts toward them. All birds consider me evil, no matter how much food I dish out. Birds don't care to be handled, to have me blow on their bellies looking for fat deposits, examine their plumage, check them for parasites. They aren't even grateful when I delicately remove ticks from their crowns or ears, or around their eyes. Only mockingbirds, and once a Baltimore oriole, greet me with happy huzzas, hopping to aviary doors as they see food (and me) approaching. And they are youngsters, who know no better, only willing to perch on my arms, or head, for a few days after they have been released. They may, however, tap on my bedroom window to rouse me at what they consider their breakfast hour for days, or even weeks.

Starlings are useful, consuming great quantities of injurious insects; there are just far too many of them. They are clannish. At my request Brad shot a male on guard at a hole in our oak tree one spring when a pair displaced the flickers nesting there. I buried the victim, and then another, every day for a week. Brad quit, but the birds didn't. When I asked at our Museum how long this could go on, I was told that one man there had shot seventy-five male replacements before he gave up. Starlings take good care of their pregnant women. Doubtless this is why they are so abundant.

The objection to them is that they drive out our native hole-nesting birds—woodpeckers, bluebirds, nuthatches, Great

Crested flycatchers, from their patiently excavated homes. Their strategy is to operate in relays, one starling on attack being replaced by a fresh one until even a larger and aggressive bird like a flicker becomes exhausted. They then toss out—or eat—any existing eggs in their prefabricated residence, and proceed to lay four or five of their own. They are a smelly bird, and I judge don't taste good either (except to Cooper's hawks). I have collected them to feed to injured owls, but even the Great Horned, after sampling a couple, will refuse them.

They forage in the open—lawns, fields, roadsides, not in woods. Flying off a few at a time mornings to the country or suburbs, they return at dusk, making a beeline for their building roosts. In Washington on cold nights they would cluster on the chimney tops of row houses near us—an untidy, restless black fringe huddled for warmth.

Cooper's hawks, according to Dr. Meng, eat them. But Cooper's are not common (one authority suggesting because there are no longer that many small birds to feed on in normal Cooper territory.) They raise—Cooper's—a brood of four or five hungry young. Interestingly, they often nest sympatrically with Solitary vireos. I have taken two of these latter here—my first—in the last few days, and seen a third. But I am not going to see or net many other migrants if a Cooper's is building in this sycamore grove. I am dismayed.

(Note: Evidently my frequent appearances discouraged the home-builder. I saw him afterward only far up under the Rhyolite Cliffs. Thank goodness! He is a magnificent flyer, though, swooping high in that bowl of air.)

In late afternoon the climbers straggle down, hot and weary. The two students have been defeated—by a turned ankle for one, and the jeans of the other are deplorably torn, so he must also have had problems. The Sierra Clubbers have lost some of their bounce, but not all. I give them iced tea until it runs out. They enthusiastically describe their routes and adventures and are off with cheerful waves. Sandy also shows up, takes my grocery list and mail, and formally asks permission to return. The English have such good manners! By the time I have done the chores, closed the nets, and tidied the Banding Office it is dark and I am hungry again.

I catch this morning's oriole at dusk and cut him out of the net. It is too dark to find a strand pulled tight around his singing yellow throat. His matins will compensate me tomorrow as I mend the hole.

Easter, April 15th. Blue and serene

The radio promises 90 degrees. Is it a measure of the culture
of southwest Arizona that on Easter morning, on all the stations of my radio, I can get only the usual daily junky cater-
wauling music? I gave Herman my short-wave machine that
brought in Tokyo, Paris, Africa, Germany, Sweden, and a
dozen Spanish-speaking cities, but never Tucson, Houston,
California. Herman was delighted, he speaks many of the lan-
guages. This morning I wished I had it back. The Baptists in
Ecuador used to come in clearer than anyone else, always singing hymns, and surely on Easter. I think of music rising in a
flood between the lofty arches and pouring shafts of light in
Washington Cathedral, and sigh. Jonquils and iris and tulips,

azaleas and forsythia, lilies, music—what am I doing out here, so far from all I used to love and take for granted?

Never mind. My day is made memorable by two men hiking separately in to bring me friendship and Easter bounty. One is Sandy the mining engineer. On Friday he had helped me set up two new nets. (If you are getting no birds in sixteen, why not try eighteen?) He had carried equipment, improved my system. Today he brings me a walking stick equipped with a hook that will help me raise and lower the nets. Double duty. A valuable English tool, gratefully received. My other Easter Rabbit is a Tucson cardiologist and fellow Board member of National Audubon, come to discuss a new sanctuary with me. Outdoorsmen both, easy and interesting companions, and fortunately compatible.

I put that useful card table on the Big House porch and pick a bowl of Peggy's Talisman roses. Brendan cooks the steak and corn and mushrooms he has brought on the rusting grill that once must have served fifty—two hundred? three hundred? I tell them the stories. Sandy produces ice cream from an insulating wad of newspapers. I fetch my hoard of frozen raspberries. There are no birds in the nets—doubtless they are off celebrating the holy day in their own rites of ancient spring fertility, festivals that long preceded our Easter. We watch a pair of Western kingbirds bluff and fight each other, establishing territory. A female also watches from a branch, judging their capabilities in her own way. Swallows hawk in the open yard. The Canyon wren slips in and out under the door carrying Easter dinner to his mate, now incubating five eggs. The phoebe, again holding feathers in her bill for the nest over our heads, fusses, then decides we mean her no harm.

Furling the nets alone at dusk, I take at last four birds. I wish the English ringer were here to admire in hand the two kingbirds we had watched. They were still fighting, oblivious of a net until it was too late. A final Easter gift, new to my list, was a seven-gram (that's about a quarter of the weight of a square of baking chocolate) Lucy's warbler, named for the daughter of an eighteenth-century zoologist. Not much larger was a warbler familiar to me in the east as a Nashville, although here it may wear four other names, depending on its race. In this part of Arizona it is a Virginia. Named for the widow of the man who secured the first specimen. You can see I have been reading again. Why not? I have plenty of time.

I haven't caught any unusual birds. This must be a considerable disappointment to those who sent me up here. It is to me.

April 17th

When pushed you fudge, and hope to get away with it. Bill
has brought visitors. The birders follow my every footstep,
which frets me. I don't want them to discover they know more
than I do (usually they do), I am supposed to be an Expert. To
my relief we reach a netted bird. They crowd close, watching
me untangle a tinier flycatcher than ever I have seen. I tell
them this. I have no idea what it is, but hope my ignorance
doesn't show.

They cry in delight, "Then it must be the Beardless!"

And so it proves. I try to act as if I take them every day.
Cupping it in closed hands I carry it to the group sunning on
the porch. They are suitably impressed. Even Bill. So am I.
My first, my only Beardless, ever. So called because all other
flycatchers have whiskers.

April 18th. Letter to John C. Ogden in California, where he is working to save the condors

"I am having a second cup of coffee to warm my cold hands. High near 83 degrees, the Tucson radio just informed me, but it has a way to climb here in the mountains. I am watching an oriole try to figure out how to get at sugar water from a pickle jar, a pyrrhuloxia breakfast out of the grain feeder, and reading a letter from those girl Rangers in my Homestead cottage. They tell me a turtle in my pond grabbed a Sharpshin by the leg, and had a magnificent, day-long meal. Must have been a Snapper. Your hens are living in my aviary. The girls are going broke feeding White-winged Doves. Wish I had some here— I am too high.

"Now the weather has improved I am getting some company. Human, there is not much in the way of migrants. Bill Roe tells me that Allan Phillips and Gale Monson can't agree on which *Selasphorus* female I took in February, but it is a state record, whichever it is. My only real accomplishment of the winter.

"I had some Leasts last week—flycatchers come through in numbers. Had the dickens of a time checking emarginate primaries, measuring tarsi, etc. I keyed them out by Phillips's system, then by Bud Lanyon's, then by Chan's. Didn't learn until too late that I should have squeezed one for the experts to study for themselves, as they aren't listed for Arizona. They are for New Mexico, though, and one recently was reported seen in Phoenix, so maybe Old Mother Fisk is right. Yesterday my only bird *all day* was a Beardless. Fortunately Bill was here to corroborate it.

"When I whine about running nets thirteen hours a day and getting so few birds—remember that October morning in Homestead when you stopped by and helped me with *two hundred* before you went to work?—Bill just chuckles and talks about where he is going to install me next winter.

"Not until February or March, I tell him. My sweaters are worn (and torn) thin. Not until I have access by eastern standards.

"The road up from the highway has finally been fixed by a seventy-year-old with an eighty-year-old helper who was born down valley and must have been suckled by a coyote. They used dynamite, compressors, a backhoe, a bulldozer—$900. worth. As an Easter gift they fetched me down to my car and proudly watched me ease up the first hundred yards. I got stuck immediately. They had only backhoed loose dirt into gullies and fissures. You can imagine what will happen in the first rain! They shoveled me out and on. With great care and grinding teeth I made it the rest of the way. Would rather have walked. If it does rain I am to rush out, even in the middle of the night, and take the car back to where it lived all winter. Frontier life . . .

"A deer went through the oriole net today so I am not as happy as I used to be to see these lovely creatures high-tailing on the ridges. They come at sunset to drink from the overflow at the water tank, if you can imagine overflow in mid-April in Arizona. Resident peacocks drive me crazy. It is spring, their gonads make them edgy. They honk and holler all day and all night—at the wind, a blown leaf, the squirrels, me, each other, nothing. They are pretty gorgeous-looking, though. From the front.

"How are the condors doing?"

April 19th

The phoebes have laid their first egg. (Unless it is a cowbird's, they are often in the yard) I now count nine species singing on territory. I have seen Brown towhees (the Spotted ones are scarce) copulating. The peacocks chase each other tirelessly all day long—around the bushes, across the porches and wood-piles, over the roofs. The horses keep knocking down the net in Sycamore Canyon that Sandy Hill helped me set up. They don't tear it, just kick out the guy lines every night as they frolic by, which drops poles and net into leaves and trash that must be cleaned out, frazzling my patience. I have brought it home, it caught nothing anyway. The half-height one I set for sparrows in a small clearing edged with thorn bushes has been irretrievably torn up. A road runner? Nothing smaller could create that much damage and I don't smell skunk. I spent an hour mending a hawk tear this morning. Wonder what he was after?

To reward me a green snake slithered across the road, glid-ing from the cave that was once an old mine entrance—there is an official paper in a bottle at its mouth. I've been warned not to explore the several small caves, because of rattlers. This snake was three to four feet long, a real beauty, moving in serpentine loops. Not grass-green, olive; not dry and dusty, but sleek. No visible markings. I had a good look, but unless it is a common species I'll bet those darned University men won't accept the sighting. My camera was back in the cabin. (Note: Of course they demanded photographic proof!)

April 21st

A second phoebe egg. A Black-headed grosbeak, having bitten my finger painfully, bumbled around one of the sugar syrup jars but failed to find the open top. And I keep saying birds are as smart as people. . . . Of course birds bite me, and scratch; and fly off jeering if I relax my hold on them for a moment. These are their only methods of defense. If I insist on handling them I must take the consequences. I've never had any health problems, except for a Short-tailed hawk that sent me briefly to a hospital with puncture wounds. My city friends expect me to come down with encephalitis, blood poisoning, heaven knows what. My only real difficulty was a catbird toenail that broke off in my thumb once and roamed around for months. The doctors couldn't locate it; they practically chewed the thumb apart, hunting.

Letter to Ann Gaylord

"That attractive friend Bix Demaree you sent to me got up at an ungodly hour and drove all the way from Phoenix. I hadn't even made my bed when she arrived with two ladies, I was washing my floor. She brought me fresh asparagus, broccoli, lemons from her own tree, wine, comfort, delight—the last the finest. It was marvelous having such companionable birders here all day. Thank you. They saw a Calliope hummer. Doggone, I missed it. It would have been a life bird for me.

"My net patrol committee, self-appointed, now consists of a Cooper's Hawk nesting somewhere nearby and doubtless feeding young; a gray fox Bix saw that I also have seen, chasing the cottontail rabbits I so enjoy (my lettuce bed garden is safely inside my banding office); the peacocks, of course; two horses who walk through nets only if I set them across their paths, and only once; deer ditto, but more than once; and a road runner.

"The mesquite has barely budded, so $200 worth of nets have rotted in the sun. I take an average of six birds a day. That's about a bird per mile walked.

"Now that the weather is a travel agent's truth, and word has gone out that the road is passable, I am getting more visitors. Fine by me. "Passable" is not used in an eastern context; an Easterner's idea of a road is something else. My car is finally at the Ranch until it rains—then I must rush it back down over the fords. I hope this doesn't happen in the dead of night, it was all I could do to drive it up here in daylight. Some Sierra Clubbers who tried to come up in a normal car ripped their drip pan, had to hike five miles to the highway and then hitch twenty to a telephone. You see why I don't get to the art galleries you ask about.

"In spite of everything I've enjoyed the winter. Beats chewing on my fingers in Homestead, watching Sharpshins take my buntings; beats going to meetings, working for charity groups in wintry Cape Cod. I'm told I've made two state records, and I've become accustomed to taking all those measurements on Empidonaces and then making a wild guess as to what they are.

"Put a sandwich in your freezer—any kind but peanut butter—for May 12th. *Deo volente.* I'm going to have to get my car put back together and all its bolts tightened after racketing it around on these boulders."

April 22nd

Inundated with company, I am not getting paperwork done. Thursday the three ladies from Phoenix; yesterday a field trip of The Nature Conservancy—a group ranging from a toddler to senior citizens. They spread out over the slopes, the canyons, and the trails to the Peak, with butterfly nets, binoculars, botany books, and broad smiles. They kept the phoebe away from her nest all day. There were climbers with pitons and ropes, too; and Larry the Botanist, who remained. After everyone had gone he and I sat out on the porch with our late supper and a bottle of wine, Bill having remembered at last to bring up a corkscrew. We ate by starlight and a lamp in clear and absolute (and welcome) silence, except for the peacocks, who yodeled at every chair scrape. I marvel that fox haven't eaten these birds, they are slow-moving. And tasty, I'm told: I haven't tried. It is the fox that is into my syrup feeders at night, licking empty the jars set out for orioles and grosbeak. The Spoffords solved this mystery at Cave Creek Canyon where, besides some eighteen hummingbird feeders hanging from wires and their roof, they daily fill a dozen small pickle jars, discovering that a surprising number of species come to them.

Accidentally one night they flashed a light on their yard and saw a fox, licking busily. They say the ringtails do the same. It's expensive. Sally must drive sixty miles to Douglas to buy sugar, so she is not pleased. In the Adirondacks I used to watch chipmunks lick at my tubular feeders, as gray squirrels do at my current home on Cape Cod, until they are empty (the tubes, not the squirrels). The chipmunks were cute, clinging to the stake the feeder was on until the last drop had been sucked. What could I do, unless I shot them? Who am I to shoot a fellow creature? He belongs in this world, too. All hobbies are expensive.

April 23rd

I leave my nets furled. Larry is going to guide me to where the trail starts up the Peak, I haven't been able to find it. He branches off before we reach the area of my confusion.

"Follow the stream bed," he tells me, shouldering his plant press.

Yesterday's returning climbers told me, "Follow all the footsteps. It's easy."

I find footsteps everywhere, mostly of cows. There are three stream beds, none of them easy walking, all of them complete with cows. One cow is wider than the trail, and six cows are impassable. Oh well—I was not going far anyway; I have other, shorter hikes in mind.

As I am opening nets Sandy the Engineer eases his truck into the parking lot, this time bringing a full quart of ice cream into which I happily dig at 8:00 A.M. Some hikers arrive, festooned with equipment and eagerness. I bring Sandy up to date, we look fruitlessly in mesquite thickets for the nest of a singing Crissal thrasher, he goes off up shady Sycamore Creek and I set to mending a net.

It is hot. For three days smog in the valley has been creeping up from the desert. I work in the shade of oaks, the small songs of small birds hidden in leaves falling about me. It is a good life, I think, though whether it is the company, the sturdy breakfast, or the ice cream that refreshes my spirits I can't decide. Rancher has not been here for three weeks, he is in Texas. Nor Herman. The peacock grain gave out a week ago, the birds follow me everywhere unhappily. But they must survive on their own when no one is here, so I try not to notice.

Well past dark I have my supper— leftover chicken salad, leftover broccoli, homegrown lettuce and herbs from my own greenhouse, all in one cold delicious dish. Because I haven't that many dishes, because one is enough to wash, because I have a lot of paperwork to finish in this, my final week. As a bonus I finish also the frozen end of the carrot cake I packed in a month ago.

I work at papers for two hours, then go out to furl net tops I had left open. I watch for rattlesnakes on the paths—it has been 80 degrees for the last few days. If you ask me, rattlesnakes are a myth. Bill's father must have marked him for life taking him as a child to a snake farm. The verbena and the white evening primroses, big as teacups, are fragrant. No owls, thank Iitoi. However could I extract them at night? They are difficult enough by daylight. Hundreds of dried oak blossoms fallen in the evening breeze sheathe the nets. Millions of brilliant stars sheathe the black sky. The peacocks, seeing my flashlight and hearing me open the gate, stir in their sleep and murmur. They are used to me. An hour ago a predator must have passed, for they honked furiously.

I stop at the Big House to get an egg for breakfast. The phoebe on her two eggs is watchful, but trusting. Before those precious eggs were laid she would have spooked and flown, but now she sits tight, regarding me with bright eyes. Back in the cabin I reach for a bowl to put the last of Sandy's ice cream in. A small mouse hops out of it. Sweet dreams . . .

April 24th

New birds all week; not many, but enough to revivify me.
The temperature ranges from 56 degrees to 84 degrees. There
are two species of cowbirds in the yard, using the old electric
pole for a lookout, joining the peacocks at meals. The books
say they especially parasitize brilliant Hooded orioles. These
have also arrived, and are singing nearby. I catch a couple of
cowbirds and consider wringing their necks, but I am here to
observe, not to manage the bird population. I'm tempted,
though. A baby oriole to me is worth far more than a baby
cowbird, which will push proper tenants out of the nest. This
is a subjective decision. That's the way ranchers feel about the
"varmints" that interfere with *their* values.

Enjoying a second cup of coffee out of doors I watch the
phoebes run a pair of violet-green swallows out of the yard.
This open area, plus the space over the corrals and water tanks,
belongs to the phoebes—just the right size, evidently, to provide food for them and their young. No swallows need tres-
pass. The phoebes do not bother the cowbirds, even when these

usurp their lookout. Cowbirds are primarily grain-eaters; there is not, evidently, competition for the food supply.

When I look a thousand feet above the avian argument I see where I was at this time yesterday. Now that I can count on my fingers the days I have left—those books I brought to read, those lazy hours lying in a deck chair, those hikes I planned . . . my time is almost gone, and what have I done? The days are crowding in on me.

High in that rhyolite massif, fissured, jagged, walling my northeastern horizon, are two large windows showing blue sky through them. These are big enough, Rancher tells me, so that ancient oaks grow in them. An eagle nested in their branches. I have seen a stunning photograph of them, I want one for myself. The day I climbed to the western horizon I figured out where I might succeed, passing from ridge to ridge, to reaching within camera distance. It has been hot, 80 degrees and more at noon the last few days, but if I started early I could go and come before the sun cooked me entirely. It is a lot quicker climbing when not swaddled in woollen layers the way I was in December.

So off I went, with orange and thermos and camera and binoculars and staff, stopping at the top of the first ridge to investigate a thrasher's grassy nest in a cholla. Close enough to peer into the spiked yellowish antlers, I found three nests of various ages. The thrashers have put this lone bush to good use. Cholla is uncommon at this elevation. *Opuntia tetracantha?* Where is Larry the Botanist? I don't go near enough chollas to become familiar with them, the result of once riding a horse though an aggregation of them.

Halfway to my distant goal I saw that if I had had the wit to mount the steep slope behind the corrals I could have had a short, straight shot at it. I comforted myself that it would have been too sunny and hot by that route. Where I was the sun was still behind the Rhyolite Cliffs and although I was sweating with effort the air was cool. A prevalent weed seemed firmly anchored in the shale so that, pushing on my staff with one hand and hauling myself up by weeds with the other, I went forward faster than I slipped back, and came to the base of the Cliff, heavily edged with oaks where water seeps down to nourish them.

I sat gratefully on a fallen silvered trunk, hoping it did not harbor scorpions or snakes, ate my orange and considered how I might get over, under, or through the taut, barbed-wire cattle fence beside me. Under seemed to be the answer as I found a spot where debris could be dug aside.

Never put your hands where you can't see, I have been warned. The size and ugliness of scorpions (and occasional black widow spiders) lurking under stones at the Ranch have led me to appreciate the warning. But my counselors weren't having to cross this fence that impeded my progress. With only a small rip to my shirt I squirmed under it.

Immediately I met a worse barrier. Across my way angled a deep arroyo I couldn't see until I reached its lip. My knees rebelled. I bit my thumb. There had to be a way. Maybe if I went higher, pushing through the oaks, to the very base of the cliff where sluicing rain had washed away all soil?

I edged along the rock face and found an animal trail made for just my purpose. Not by cows—it was too narrow, and clean. There were no horse droppings, no deer sign, no uprooted lechuguilla the javelina strew around. No lechuguilla at all, thank goodness. The trail slipped through high mountain grass like the path a cat leaves in the tall grass of a farm field. Mountain lion? How I want to see one! I've read they are curious about humans, not vicious. If they had laid out this trail they had used good judgment, circling under gnarled oak limbs here, around a mammoth boulder there, down a little, up more.

I was still in shadow, still cool, placing my feet carefully. A sunny hillock lay dead ahead, I should be directly under those window arches. Finding footing flat enough to look up I did, and found an overhanging cliff entirely blocked my objective. A scarlet-blooming cactus hung off one side of this. Sullenly I photographed it instead, for my memory book. Then I climbed on—too late to turn back—the sun hot on my shoulders now, the footing hazardous. Baboquivari seemed hardly a hand's breath away in the crystalline air. Mexico showed in a haze over the southern ridges, now below my line of sight for the first time. I could follow my lifeline to civilization as it wound and twisted far distant. No vehicle coming up it. No vehicle driver could ever see me.

On a bit. The arches emerged, foreshortened, undramatic. How stupid of me! Of course that picture I coveted had been taken from a plane, flying level with them. Oh well.

I sat on a rock, transferring the cold lemonade in the thermos on my back to my front. Disappointed and hot I wondered, What is the urge that makes people—me—want to climb every hill in sight? To get away from a prosaic daily round? A good book, a couple of sherries would do the same. To put those daily rounds in perspective, to look from a distance at life in the hope of seeing a pattern, as, looking down at the Ranch, I observe how orderly its layout is, astonishingly different from my ground's-eye view as I walk about through its uneven footing and peacocks?

A release of spirit? Or is climbing just the physical thrill of conquest, the satisfaction of stretching our bodies to find where their limits are? My desire for a photograph of those windows was only a rationalization. I was not really weary. If I had wanted to I could have hunted a cleft in the cliffs above me, perhaps have mounted to their summit. But for what? A view of different ridges. Was my enjoyment on that rock a wisdom come with age? Twenty years ago would I have sat so peacefully, letting the crystal air lighten my bones? Or did I pass that urgent stage of activity as a child, climbing up and down our local New Hampshire mountain all one summer, finding nothing at its summit but another view, another water-lily pond (complete with leeches).

A woodpecker drummed. The descending notes of a Canyon wren fell from the cliffs above me, an oriole's melody mounted sweetly from below. This whole airy world was mine. And Iitoi's.

I realized without surprise that I have abandoned wondering Why Am I Here? I have abandoned my hope of listing new birds for the area, of sending down reports to excite my sponsors, of making some small reputation in ornithology for myself. My sponsors seem satisfied to have me doing what little I am. Perhaps I have earned this peaceful end to my life. (I doubt this.) If I died tomorrow I would die content.

Who is ever contented? After a while, sated with sun and scenery, not to mention pseudothinking, I embarked on my descent. The way down looked easy —broad slopes, a few oaks scattered here and there. No cows, though; no cow paths. Odd. What I didn't see, looking down, were broken rock shelves hidden by heavy vegetation, stony slides, everywhere cactus of a half-dozen kinds. I had to make my way with great care, I am expecting no visitors who would search for me. The sun blazed. The nearer I came to the Creek the more appalling were the pitches. No wonder there were no cow paths! This is what I had thought I might climb, or descend so easily?

When staff and footing slipped at the same time I slithered painfully on my rear. It is well padded, but once I really fell. By a miracle my precious binoculars dangled in front, but I heard camera and thermos crunch in the backpack. I didn't crack (I think today) my shoulder blade; it seems lame and bruised only. I'll know about the camera when its film emerges. My precious photographs of birds! Drat those windows above me, and my athletic ambitions!

But although I slid frequently into prickly purple thistles, and plenty of cat's claw, not once did I land in the abundant cactus. Was it by courtesy of the Papago gods so close, appreciating my love for their land? My pauses to savor its splendor, to photograph its flowers, the fishhook cactus that twist on their bases, seeking the sun? to listen to its bird song and singing winds? I came safely at last to the trail along the Creek.

Clear of the rocks and vegetation, able to see my feet again, I saw my toes had pressed through the tips of my sneakers. They were the old ones, though, worn five months. Pretty good.

The lack of drama through my winter must be a disappointment to my friends who think in terms of High Adventure. Not to my family, though, nor to The Nature Conservancy, who will be stuck with my care if I break a bone, am attacked by a lion or a wetback, bust my car and have to buy a new one, slip—this is more likely—somewhere on these slopes, not to be found for a week.

With time and routine life becomes humdrum wherever you are. I now take for granted the small inconveniences, the beauty, the quiet, the daily events that so stimulated me when first I arrived. There doesn't seem much to write about, really. The diary I kept for a while is discarded. I have grown accustomed to the bird species, although every new blooming flower enthralls me. I notice what is about, but it doesn't seem worth recording. I haven't had to rush out in the night in rain to drive my car down the dark canyon, making an equally onerous way back by flashlight. I haven't knocked over a candle or set things on fire with that ever-burning wood stove, nor run out of propane. I wasn't here the day the Rescue Squad took four overenthusiastic young people off the Peak, or at least I was here only for the beginning and no one had time for coffee or conversation.

Frankly I am bored today.

Undated

I wish someone would figure out how far I walk every day. There is the loop from the cabin that runs behind the Big House, across Horse Bars Creek, up Sparrow Hill, down a small arroyo, down across a wash where the horses walk at night, dumping close alongside my two nets but never tearing them. That's where I caught the owls. Then up Primrose Hill to the water tanks, through a gate and back into the yard where the junco net was and the peacocks are waiting for breakfast. For a while I had a spur through another gate into cattle country by the verdin's nest. It was an extra haul, but I miss it. Then through the back yard, the gate by the outhouse, across the Creek, almost dry; up the stone steps Audubon built, over the hill on the horse trail to Sycamore Canyon and its dry creekbed where Broad-tailed hummingbirds are now nesting. I do the near loop again before eating breakfast. How far is all this? A mile? Three-quarters? How often do I do it? Ten times a day? More? I mean to keep track, but I forget. If I had a bookkeeper's mind I wouldn't be doing this sort of work, that's for sure. Six miles a day, eight, ten? My legs know. Maybe it's just as well I don't.

My trouble is, I like words. Day after day, no one to talk with, I talk to myself, string words together as I run the nets. Using as subjects the flowers that have come into bloom along my paths, wind in the new mesquite leaves, the horses thumping the ground as they canter off, the cattle grouped, staring, by a fence. Shifting a word here and there; adding, subtracting, until their sounds and shapes satisfy me. When you are alone your interior landscape is as important as the exterior, so I also build stories in my head about what I think and feel— all discarded when finally I find a bird in a net and must concentrate on picking out claws and wings while its bill hammers on my thumb, its eyes watch me, bright with apprehension. Perhaps this is why I can't remember, however often I plan to try, how many times I run my routes.

I leave paragraphs in the air behind me as I do footprints in the sands of the Creek. Like the footprints, a few of them may last and get written down in the evenings—a form of doodling to occupy me once I have recorded the day's meager scientific data, while the lamp hisses and the mice rustle.

I didn't plan to write this journal. It arrived uninvited, like a stray dog by my stove, demanding attention, nourishment; offering companionship. Phrases turning around and around, like a dog underfoot—under my tongue, under my hand, until finally they and I became comfortable together. I'll pitch these pages out before I leave, there are other words back East. Only there I am busier, I haven't time to play. (Note: Many months later I found these doodles. My helpful friends had packed them the day they came to move me out. It seemed a shame to waste them. Bit by bit with nostalgia, my letters to Sally, the notes on my worksheets, they grew into a book. Again just a doodle, a bigger one, to occupy me winter evenings at a Biological Station where I was working.)

I am not the only one who uses the trail to Sycamore Canyon. This afternoon I am guiding a visitor. As we start up the slope a mouse comes racing toward us, feet flying until it meets our human feet and leaps frantically aside. Is a fox after it? I see fox over here, chasing rabbits. So far the rabbits have come out ahead, at least while I am watching. Or did a deer startle this mouse? One stands, ears pricked, off in the mesquite.

"Do you often see deer?" my visitor asks, checking his steps.

I answer casually, without thinking, "Yes, almost every time I come over here."

He murmurs to himself, "Imagine living where you see deer every day!" and stands until the animal bounds off.

I am embarrassed. I *am* lucky. I stoop and show him the

mariposa lilies just coming into bloom, the tiny, ground-hug-ging euphorbia with its intricate pattern. I point out the many butterflies feeding on thistles and miniature wildflowers, themselves miniature; a stump where Acorn woodpeckers nested until a squirrel found them. I give him everything I can think of from the rich and fortunate life I lead to make up for his having to live in a city. He carries back, in the nylon mesh bags I sew for this purpose, two birds we find netted. Their small claws prick his fingers.

In the Banding Office I hold one of these, a flycatcher, in my hand, its eyes watching us alertly. As long as my hold is firm it does not struggle or show signs of fright. Let my fingers relax for a moment, though, as I reach for pliers and the cor-rectly sized band, and I will have lost it. It will be out the door and gone, or up in the rafters seeking escape—now dart-ing behind furniture, now taking refuge in plants as I swear and try to retrieve it. I have a long-handled net for this pur-pose but must be careful not to damage a wing. A bird is quicker by far than I am. If I cannot herd it into a corner, or net it fluttering against the screen, I open the door and let it go.

Some, I tell my companion, are gone before the door is wide. House sparrows and starlings are the smartest. (These are eastern observations; a bird rarely escapes me here, they are too scarce and precious.) Catbirds, Black-throated blue war-blers, and a few others lack the wit to fly low out the door. They will flutter high against the ceiling, until dusk makes the door contrastingly bright.

A panicked antique dealer on Cape Cod once sent for me. A catbird was trapped in his showroom, a renovated barn with windows too high to open. Catbirds are fruit-eaters, their droppings purple (one reason I wear blue jeans). Lacking a hungry Sharp-shinned or Cooper's hawk, I had to tell him that only sunset and an open door would remove his equally panicked visitor. I made no friend for wildlife.

This flycatcher is dressed in soft grays and yellow. The brown marks across its tail say it is the Ash-throated. As any fossil-minded or well-instructed schoolchild can tell you, birds are descended from Archaeopteryx, a lizard that evolved heavy wings for gliding. The scales on this bird's legs and feet are identical with the scaly skin of some reptiles. Its horny bill is similar to turtle jaws. Don't be insulted, Little Lady in my Hand, you are far prettier, and a far better flier. After millions of years Archaeopteryx has become this airy-boned structure that brightens our landscape and feeds on injurious insects. If we could see under those soft feathers, manipulate the skeletal bones, we would find that her skull articulates with its vertebrae not as ours and other mammalian skulls do but with a pronounced similarity to reptiles.

She is warm-blooded, like us. She uses her energy far faster than we do. My visitor listens to her heartbeat—rapid, like a little motor. His beats about 72 times a minute, I tell him. A cardinal's heartbeat is 391—higher when it is angrily biting my fingers! A Ruby-throat's at rest is 614, and it breathes 250 times a minute, astronomically multiplied in flight, thought to be correlated to its wingbeats. If Bill Roe used up as much energy as a hummingbird does, Alice would have to feed him 155,000 calories a day. If he weighed only 170 pounds. No wonder doctors try to keep us thin. If a hummingbird ran out of liquid it might ignite. A bird's life is chancy.

When you plant your grounds, I admonish my visitor, new to Arizona, plant berry-bearing shrubs for the thrush family; calendulas and composites for finches and seed-eaters; but remember the many western hummingbirds and add nectar-throated flowers for them. Birds are up early, eager for break-fast long before you go out to fill your feeders. (He has been complaining about the dawn chorus in his yard waking him.) That's why, after the forty minutes it takes me to open the nets at first light, no matter how hungry I am I run my route a second time before breakfast, to make sure no small and also hungry creature is caught.

I band the flycatcher and let it go to refuel. I take my visitor to my cabin for cheese and beer, to refuel him.

April 25th

Off to Ohio for an Audubon meeting. It will be eastern spring with every wildflower of that climate blooming around Marie Aull's home, spilling down slopes into the greening woods, fragrant along the brooks. Her gardens are famous and open to all, so natural that you are barely aware of the years of planning gone into them. The love shows, though, as it shows in the face of this small, energetic woman responsible for an Audubon educational program that serves a large community. The years we are fortunate enough to meet at her Center we break business by going out at dusk and listening to the courting woodcocks that plummet, whistling, at our feet. We lap up Marie's peasant soup and crusty bread, see the one-acre sample of a prairie that once stretched to the horizon. Our world can't be evil when it has Marie Aulls in it.

Before I leave I take trash to the dump, shake out Gene's rug, mop the floor. If some careless teen-ager or beer-blurry driver crumps me on the highway I want everything left tidy. Astonishingly, at twilight a brilliant Hooded oriole and an equally bright Scott's fly to the fig tree at the Big House and perch one above the other in the bare branches, sing vespers. As their duet continues it becomes for me a distillation of all the clarity and beauty of spring in this remote canyon.

> As if the earth in one unlooked for favor
> Had made them certain earth returned their love.

Unlike the two listeners on Robert Frost's wooded mountain I am alone on mine, listening for all people to this evening antiphony. This is a gift, a trust I am being given to carry to those who can hear only the sounds of our technological culture.

Scattered clouds over the ridges turn from apricot to gray to moonlit white as I secure my nets for four days against wind and weather. I extricate from the last one, which has not caught a bird in weeks, a Say's phoebe. By feel, it is now dark. When you have handled 40,000 birds your fingers are your eyes. (Well—an easy one I can get out. Otherwise I run for a flashlight.) Usually a late bird like this I keep screened in my Banding room, safe from things that may go pounce in the night on a creature not yet settled in its roost. But this phoebe has not far to go—only around the corner of the house, to join its mate at that nest on the porch rafter.

Study birds and you learn history—fringe benefit. Over supper I read that the name Say's on my phoebe commemorates an entomologist who accompanied Major Stephen H. Long's expedition to the Rockies in 1819. But the fringe benefit that has mattered to me this day—this week—this spring— is the song of those two orioles rising in the air of dusk to Iitoi on his Peak above us.

April 30th

After four days' absence I circle my property to see what has gone on. Even without the note taped to my door by a Band-Aid I would recognize my visitors. The horse bars are down—that would be Rancher Brother, forgetful (we all have our small weaknesses). Rancher has brought 100 pounds of grain for the peacocks. Carefully he took down and coiled a mist net that might have been in the way of the propane truck. Which has not come: there are no tracks and the gauge is still in the red Danger Zone. I had better bathe in the outdoor shower back of my cabin if I am to have functioning fridges and a stove until I leave the end of the week.

Maybe I should bathe in that gallon of milk Peggy brought me? I'll not be able to drink it all. She also thoughtfully brought me a head of lettuce. Unbagged, it is wilting, as are the unwatered scarlet blooms of the petunias hung where peacocks cannot get at them. Probably she never notices hummingbirds zooming in and out to the flowers. She is not an animal woman, although a fine cat catcher. She left two hoses running on her gardens (hers or the peacocks?—the iris buds all are eaten) but she did not fill the shallow pans scattered about for their water, nor clean algae from the deep ones. No problem with water, the tank still overflows.

Peggy is also a passionate cleaner. Not inside, for the grease I had swabbed at but not conquered is still on the kitchen floor (I am not so hot indoors myself). Each time she comes her first act is to sweep the peacock dung off the Big House porch, and hose it down.

Someone has dug a hole under the cement slab of my porch. Someone else—or the same—has entered, and eaten those withered apples on my windowsill. Ground squirrels have ravaged the feeders. They, or a fox, knocked the last of the sugar jars to the ground, breaking it. Before I hurried away I must have spilled hummingbird syrup on my kitchen counter. As I enter a swarm of ants rushes off. Sharing works both ways.

At dark, returning my supper supplies to the Big House fridge, I flick my flashlight toward the phoebe nest to wish my friends good night. No bright eye shines at me.

NO ONE IS THERE! NO NEST, NOTHING! *Not a straw, not a twig!* The rafter is as bare as if it had been scrubbed. *Hosed!*

Rancher told me that the phoebes have nested on that rafter for the ten years he has been here. Has Peggy destroyed their home each spring? Has she wiped out the young of these gentle, useful creatures that share our world, that all through this long winter have been my companions? Those five eggs were due to hatch. The cowbirds, scratching their high notes from the electric pole, had not found the nest. All the excrement from five bird chicks up to the time of their fledging would barely equal one of those damned peacock droppings I am forever stepping in.

I am not a woman who weeps. People are different, I tell myself. Creatures smaller than a cat or a hen are of no importance to many, go unrecognized. But as I return to my cabin both my feet and my heart are heavy. Where are those phoebes, grieving as I grieve, tonight?

(Note: May 5th, the day I left, I saw the birds carrying nesting material to the side of the house that rises straight from Horse Bars Creek—a place Peggy would never see, nor be able to reach. There were five old nests there, lined up on a rafter. So this is an annual destruction and resurgence. For what comfort this can give me.)

May Day

In the noon sun, I stand in the yard gazing at Baboquivari, at the clefts and fissures, the shifting colors that soften its harsh majesty. It is my familiar. There for how long? And it will be there for millions of years after I am gone. While it affects my moods, often hourly, it is not aware of me. I am reminded of what Hal Borland wrote in *Countryman: A Summary of Belief*.

> Fundamentally, man is a minor creature on the face of the earth, . . . bigger than a fox but smaller than a cow . . . vastly outnumbered everywhere by the mice, by the grasshoppers, by the birds. . . . My footsteps will mark a path across the land, proof of my presence here: but ten minutes after I am gone the grass will grow again where I walked and the rain will smooth the sand where I knelt to plant or drink. . . . The fox and the hawk, the maple tree and the briar, will have no recollection of my ever having lived.

Neither of us is depressed by this, just realistic. Please note his remark on mice.

People fret about my living alone here in the shadow of Baboquivari. I am hardly alone when I have Hal Borland and Edward Abbey and a dozen similar companions—and all that mail. I should be inside, thanking my friends for their concern. But nights are for inside. I can't bear to miss an instant of outside, even if I am only washing out the ash bucket.

Perched in branches above the chicken coop the peacocks watch me languidly. To them I am only Cinderella, scattering grain. When I leave they, and "their moonlight and the rising of their sun"—again I borrow from Mr. Borland—"will not be altered one iota by my having been here."

Never mind, *I* will remember. Tranced in the heat and light, I stand imprinting the mountain on my eyes. If I could have had this experience when I was twenty . . . if I could have learned to handle myself as I have had to here, to find my values, to discover the rocks, metaphorical as well as real, that would slide under me, as against the ones set solidly. I was a scaredy-cat, knowing barely enough to change a lightbulb, leaning on my father, on Brad. What would my life have been like? I would have had a strength, a stronger discipline for the children I spoiled. Life would have been easier, surely, for Brad.

An inner voice interrupts sharply: You are maundering. What have you done here for yourself? What about Bill and Herman and the Ranchers and Scott? Alice doing your shopping for you? You've had jeeps and firewood, fresh broccoli and ice cream and all those visitors. Don't tell *me* you've been standing on your own feet. I'll admit—the voice turns grudging—you've learned a bit. But it's about time. Don't go overboard. You've been trouble to The Conservancy, have you been worth it? Stop philosophizing, it's not your forte.

Baboquivari says nothing. Hot sun pours on its granite face and on me equally; on the silken green curve of the big agaves; on the blue of jays, on the emerald tail of Peacock Primero come to see why I am so still.

Long ago I asked—you asked—WHAT AM I DOING HERE? I still don't know. It doesn't matter. Do we need excuses for being? The happiness welling through me is a gift from the high gods, a strength to carry me to whatever is the end of my days. No clock ticks. No one waits for me. In the utter silence of noon only the sun moves.

And the peacocks, come hunting Primero.

Letter to Molly

"When you get this I will have left. Four more days. There is some idea that enthusiastic William will come tomorrow to show me where he hopes I can work next winter. On the desert, not too far, on a creek in cottonwoods. (Those are trees, Sweety-pie! One word, not two. What other questions have you?) The town there is isolated every time it rains, sometimes for weeks. I was going to abandon all the kitchen gear, bedding, etc. I bought to equip this cabin, but Bill says it is to go into his cellar, I am coming back. He is a dear.

"Time to run nets again. I am getting hummingbirds, they will strangle themselves unless I keep running around to extract them. This has fixed it so I can fasten my belt again, after sitting all winter."

May 3rd

I catch a few migrants. Herman is here. I have thought all winter that he disapproved of my activities, but he is charmed by the colored scraps of warblers I now can show him, the bold and biting grosbeaks. Probably I should stay on another week in the hope of getting further species, but Least tern are flying north from South America, I have commitments in the east. I pack papers in cartons, write overdue letters, try to remove those stains I inherited in the bathtub and sink.

The worst of my clothing is packed for Rancher's charity in Nogales. The heavy carton of emergency cans brought up for visitors who never arrived, the pounds of dried beans sent me as a joke, and other foodstuffs can go to Alice and Liz. The frozen lemonade and apple juice are medicines to sustain me. My throat is too sore to swallow.

Bill and Scott appeared, and took me to a six-hundred-acre ranch in Altar Valley. Owned by the same family since before the Civil War, when this country was unsettled, it somehow escaped the fiery raids of both Spaniards and Indians. A permanent stream runs through arid mesquite flatland—a broad, sunken channel carved out and marked by cottonwoods, walnut, ash, oak, and willows two hundred and more years old. Its banks were verdant with shrubs, musical with song. The rare becard built its long shaggy nests fifty feet over our heads. A Great Horned owl contemplated us, its hoot more a vibration than a call. A Cooper's hawk carrying food to its young ignored us. Tanagers were glints of flame in the leaves. The woman who owns this glory wants it preserved, not used for housing lots that will suck up its water for dishwashers and bathrooms and highballs.

This was the spring I have yearned for all through the harsh winter. Joyfully I hopped and splashed across shallow water interlacing gravel beds, over trees torn out by floods. I was ecstatic at the number of migrants. I did not notice, in my delight, that the many old willow trees were in rampant bloom. Tree pollen! My throat closed up. The men hurried me back to where the air blew clean and clear off the mountain, but it was too late.

Next morning visitors arrived and asked Herman for the Bird Lady. When I went to greet them my mouth opened but not even a whisper came out. I am limp, lack-luster, ill. I pack, but my organization is gone. Anything I may need until I reach Massachusetts two weeks from now—telephone numbers, proper shoes, notebooks, a paring knife—becomes irretrievably lost. I fill cartons, fasten them shut, open them again. I stagger around outside gathering in the nets. Herman watches me with alarm.

May 5th

I left the heavy poles bundled for the men to carry when they arrive. Far earlier than I expected they do, bringing with them the Spoffords, who had planned to move me in five months ago and are just now getting here. I am not ready and the confusion is vast.

"Go away!" I beg them huskily. "Go hike! There is a hawk's nest in the next canyon." (Spoff is a hawk man.)

They disappear but are back too soon. They remove cartons, empty the fridge, put things into their vans before I can prevent them, so that when we reach Tucson my personal needs have gone to Cave Creek, I can't find even my toothbrush. My watch with its turquoise Indian band, my silver combs that hold unruly hair out of my eyes, where are they? I love my zealous helpers. I am grateful to them. I am too frail to manage them or care. Next week I will be wild.

Only light stuff is put into my car so I will have no trouble bouncing over that "improved road." My escorts slam their van doors and wait.

For a long, quiet moment I look. Through the sparkling air that limns every ledge and cleft of Baboquivari I look up to this backdrop of my long winter, this guardian of my days and nights. I sent my gratitude winging to the unseen spirits who have watched over me, to whatever force created this immense, brooding, gold and green weathered peak. The moment is not long enough.

Impatient horns blow. From a bed of ivy a peacock lifts its head to see why. Reluctantly I get into my car. Reluctantly, with blurred vision, I maneuver the washouts of that mountain road for the last time.

"Who can stand in the presence of a mountain," Hal Borland wrote, "and remain unchanged?"

Appendix

June

"Dear Bill and Alice, Scott and Liz:

"As you well know I bitched all winter. Not enough birds.
Rain. Cold. Snow. No carpet of flowers such as we thought
spring would surely bring. No fantastic spring migration that
everyone, not just you, pictured for me. No rare species.

"Through all of my vicissitudes, none of your making, you
patiently cared for me, fed me (blue eggs! asparagus!), photocopied my reports, brought up mail and friends, ran my
errands, educated my ignorance. I rewarded you with complaints, snarls, and an occasional beer, and could only hope
my affection showed through this critical crust.

"Now that I am back on the Atlantic coast with its pines,
terns, and resort traffic, I want to tell you that every day in
my sight looms that sun- or rain-lit bulk of Baboquivari.
Those steep slopes, those golden cliffs of rhyolite, the sweep
of valley and foothills, the miles of ocotillo that never did

blossom for me on my plods in and out, are a part of me for all of my days.

"Now that it is too late I wish to thank you for my winter. Busy with your many activities you will forget me. Bless you, and The Nature Conservancy. I shall not forget you.

Your Lady of the Mountain,

Jonnie"

BIRDS HANDLED, IN ORDER OF ABUNDANCE

Species	Handled	Repeats
*Oregon Junco (*Junco hyemalis*)	77	125 (by 63 birds)
Empidonax species	31	–
*Gray-headed Junco (*Junco hyemalis*)	26	21
Brown Towhee (*Pipilo fuscus*)	25	20
Rufous-crowned Sparrow (*Aimophila ruficeps*)	21	32 (by 15 birds)
Mexican Jay (*Aphelocoma ultramarina*)	20	18
Chipping Sparrow (*Spizella passerina*)	18	–
Black-chinned Sparrow (*Spizella atrogularis*)	17	12
Ruby-crowned Kinglet (*Regulus calendula*)	12	1
Spotted Towhee (*Pipilo maculatus*)	12	11

* The Oregon, Gray-headed, and Slate-colored Juncos have been lumped into one species, the Dark-eyed Junco (*Junco hyemalis*), by the American Ornithologists' Union in their latest (5th) *Checklist of North American Birds.* However, they are easily separable, and the Bird Banding Laboratory of the U.S. Fish & Wildlife Service requires the former classifications on the schedules I must send them. The Slate-colored is relatively uncommon in western Arizona; the Oregon far outnumbered the Gray-headed at the Ranch, and left for the north at a different time, so I have classified them separately here.

Hermit Thrush (*Catharus guttatus*)	10	15 (by 5 birds)
Solitary Vireo (*Vireo solitarius*)	10	–
Pyrrhuloxia (*Cardinalis sinuatus*)	10	4
Ash-throated Flycatcher (*Myiarchus cinerascens*)	8	3
House Finch (*Cardopacus mexicanus*)	8	–
Black-throated Sparrow (*Aimophila bilineata*)	8	3
Bewick's Wren (*Troglodytes bewickii*)	7	7 (by 4 birds)
Brown-headed Cowbird (*Molothrus ater*)	7	1
Black-chinned Hummingbird (*Archilochus alexandri*)	6	1
Costa's Hummingbird (*Calypte costae*)	6	–
Curve-billed Thrasher (*Toxostoma curvirostre*)	6	12 (by 5 birds)
Scott's Oriole (*Icterus parisorum*)	6	2
Anna's Hummingbird (*Calypte anna*)	4	–
Acorn Woodpecker (*Melanerpes formicivorus*)	4	–
Wied's Crested Flycatcher (*Myiarchus tyrannulus*)	4	–
Hutton's Vireo (*Vireo huttoni*)	4	–
Yellow-rumped Warbler (*Dendroica coronata*)	4	1
Hooded Oriole (*Icterus cucullatus*)	4	2
White-winged Dove (*Zenaida asiatica*)	3	–
Ladder-backed Woodpecker (*Dendrocopus scalaris*)	3	5 (by 2 birds)
Bridled Titmouse (*Parus wollweberi*)	3	–
Verdin (*Auriparus flaviceps*)	3	2
Canyon Wren (*Catherpes mexicanus*)	3	1
Warbling Vireo (*Vireo gilvus*)	3	–
Black-headed Grosbeak (*Pheucticus ludovicianus*)	3	–

Lesser Goldfinch (*Carduelis psaltria*)	3	–
Slate-colored Junco (*Junco hyemalis*)	3	4
Western Screech Owl (*Otus kennicottii*)	2	–
Poor-will (*Phalaenoptilus nuttallii*)	2	–
Rufous Hummingbird (*Selasphorus rufus*)	2	–
Broad-billed Hummingbird (*Cyanthus latirostris*)	2	–
Common Flicker (*Colaptes auratus*)	2	–
Gila Woodpecker (*Melanerpes uropygialis*)	2	3 (by 2 birds)
Western Kingbird (*Tyrannus verticalis*)	2	–
Say's Phoebe (*Sayornis saya*)	2	1
Western Wood Pewee (*Contopus sordidulus*)	2	–
Rock Wren (*Salpinctes obsoletus*)	2	–
Wilson's Warbler (*Wilsonia pusilla*)	2	–
Cardinal (*Richmondena cardinalis*)	2	1
Green-tailed Towhee (*Pipilo chlorurus*)	2	–
Lincoln's Sparrow (*Melospiza lincolnii*)	2	8
Road runner (*Geococcyx californianus*)	1	–
Broad-tailed Hummingbird (*Selasphorus platycercus*)	1	–
Hummingbird, unidentified female (*Selasphorus*)	1	–
Hummingbird, unidentified female (?)	1	–
Beardless Flycatcher (*Camptostoma imberbe*)	1	–
Yellow-bellied Sapsucker (*Sphyrapicus varius*)	1	1
Violet-green Swallow (*Tachycineta thalassina*)	1	–

Cactus Wren (*Campylorhynchus brun-*
neicapillus)   1   –

Crissal Thrasher (*Toxostoma crissale*)   1   –

Nashville Warbler (*Helminthophila ruf-*
icapilla)   1   –

Lucy's Warbler (*Helminthophila luciae*)   1   1

Black-throated Gray Warbler (*Den-*
droica nigrescens)   1   –

MacGillivray's Warbler (*Oporornis tol-*
miei)   1   –

Bullock's (Northern) Oriole (*Icterus*
galbula)   1   –

Bronzed Cowbird (*Molothrus aeneus*)   1   –

Western Tanager (*Piranga ludoviciana*)   1   –

Lazuli Bunting (*Passerina cyanea*)   1   –

White-crowned Sparrow (*Zonotrichia*
leucophrys)   1   –